To Rich...
Christmas 1978 with
love from Mummy

The Elegant but Easy Cookbook

THE
Elegant But Easy Cookbook

By
MARIAN FOX BURROS
and
LOIS LEVINE

REVISED EDITION

Illustrated by Rosalie Petrash Schmidt

COLLIER BOOKS

A Division of Macmillan Publishing Co., Inc.

NEW YORK

COLLIER MACMILLAN PUBLISHERS

LONDON

Library of Congress Catalog Card Number: 67-12793

FIRST COLLIER BOOKS EDITION 1968

Twelfth Printing 1977

Portions of this book appeared previously in *Elegant But
Easy*, copyright © 1960 by Marian Fox Burros and Lois
Liebeskind Levine, and in *Second Helpings*, copyright ©
1963 by Marian F. Burros and Lois L. Levine.

Macmillan Publishing Co., Inc.
866 Third Avenue, New York, N.Y. 10022
Collier Macmillan Canada, Ltd.

Printed in the United States of America

Contents

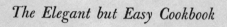

The Elegant but Easy Cookbook

Introduction

WRITING an introduction turns out to be a more difficult task than collecting, testing, and writing recipes. However, a word or two about this book may interest our readers, some of whom will remember certain parts from our previous book, titled *Elegant but Easy*.* We had our share of trials and tribulations before that book was accepted by our eventual publisher and issued in paperback form. But its acceptance by our readers has been so gratifying and continuous that we were asked to edit and expand the original version, and the result is what you are reading now. Although *Elegant but Easy* was the basis for this work, we went through it carefully, editing and deleting, but most especially adding, to make this volume as complete and useful as possible.

This new and expanded cookbook should prove as helpful

* Collier Books, 1961.

to new readers as the former has been. We dedicate it to all
those who have written to tell us they have worn their original
Elegant but Easy to shreds. (We hope *they* will replace it
with this more permanent form.) The new recipes are as
elegant to serve and easy to consume, thanks to advance
preparation by the cook, as the old ones we have retained
have proven to be. This, naturally, leads us to answer your
question, "How?"

We believe entertaining really should be fun, for the hostess
as well as the guests. The qualities of a pleasant party are
often intangible, but good company and delicious food con-
tribute a great deal to the guests' enjoyment. The hostess, too,
should be able to participate and not have to spend her time
in the kitchen cooking, tasting, and seasoning. So few of us
have help today! This does not mean, however, that every-
thing should come from the precooked or instant section of
your grocers' shelves. You can prepare *Elegant but Easy*
meals with no help and still enjoy the company of your
guests. We'd like to show you how.

Of course there must be congenial guests, and choosing a
convivial group is as important as choosing the right combination of foods. An almost scientific set of rules for select-
ing a guest list begins with the "do-nots":

DO NOT invite an entire clique or group of close friends at
one time. Rather try to add a new couple to an established
group or introduce couples you feel would enjoy each other's
company. This way, even if the talk returns to gardening or
babies, it will be new gardens and new babies.

DO NOT bunch "categories"—all your doctor friends at one
time would be deadly though antiseptic--together unless you
have a very specific purpose: a birthday, a shower, a family
gathering, a meeting of the American Medical Association!

DO NOT try to wipe out all your obligations at one fell
swoop. Guests catch on quickly to your motives and deter-
mine not to enjoy themselves!

So much for your guest list; every rule is here to be broken.

Whatever you enjoy, no doubt the rest of your company will, too. Just do not, please, have ten lawyers and one engineer!

The number of your guests, as well as the space you have available, influences your menu. For experimenting with something new invite the couple next door or your closest friends, informally. Note that many of these recipes are written for four servings. As a matter of fact, our neighbors —not to mention the authors—have grown plump helping us get together this book, as every recipe has been carefully tested and tasted! In a small apartment dinners for six or eight are probably all that can be handled comfortably for both cook and guests. If you have the room and wish to entertain twenty for dinner, a buffet—with two or three entrees—would be as effective as a formal sitdown dinner. Please, please, however, when serving a buffet, do not expect your guests to balance plates on their knees. Provide some kind of table; bridge tables are good, or those handy little stack tables that are so popular.

Whenever possible, it is fun to set a theme for your party; any happy occasion: a birthday, anniversary, new home, new job, new bride, new couple in town. Or let the menu set the theme such as a Chinese dinner, an Italian feast, a curry supper. Vary the usual party fare! Your flowers, table decor, and invitations (if you are so inclined) with your menu complete the picture.

The foods you serve need not be expensive to be *elegant* and the recipes need not be oversimplified to be *easy*. The ease comes at serving time thanks to advance preparation. Foods need not be prepared at the last minute to be impressive. Soups, though elegant, require extra dishes and often entail extra bother for the servantless hostess, who can avoid last-minute pot-watching by serving the first course in the form of hors d'oeuvres during the cocktail hour. Lobster soufflé is divine, but so is Chicken Imperial. Serve on your best platter, use your best table service and linens, and put your best foot forward. You can be confident of success thanks to careful planning. The meal is set well in advance, there are no details to be completed at the zero hour. You are a guest at your own party!

The "how-to" is the basis for this cookbook. We have incorporated many recipes for foods that can be prepared one or more days in advance and lose nothing in standing. Such recipes are designated by a "#" followed by a numeral, representing the number of days in advance such food may safely be prepared and refrigerated. Other recipes are marked with an "*" to denote that they are freezable. (For example: *#2 Chafing-Dish Meat Balls—these can either be prepared two days in advance and refrigerated, or considerably in advance and then frozen.) With the exception of a few ice-cream dishes, or unless otherwise noted, these frozen foods should be removed from the freezer the night before serving to allow ample time for thorough defrosting. We have also included some "quickies" for last minute guests.

As an example, let us prepare a formal menu and plan it to allow the hostess to be genuinely relaxed when the guests arrive.

Toasted Mushroom Rolls
Tuna-cheese Spread
Chicken Divan   *Cornflaked Potatoes*
Spinach Tart   *Orange-coconut Mold*
Heat-and-Serve Rolls
Chocolate Roll   *Coffee*

If the party is given on Saturday night, sometime before Thursday, even two or three weeks in advance, you should prepare the mushroom rolls, chicken and chocolate roll. Wrap and freeze.

Do your marketing Wednesday. Thursday make the mold, the potatoes. Friday make the spinach tart, and the tuna spread. Your refrigerator may bulge a bit, but it will be very, very empty on Sunday.

Saturday, the day of the party, set the table, defrost the chicken, chocolate roll and mushroom rolls. Then take a nap! An hour before the guests arrive, fix the pot for coffee. One-half hour before, set the mushroom rolls on a cookie sheet, ready to pop in the oven as soon as the first guests arrive. Reheat the chicken, brown the rolls and potatoes in the oven. You are really all set as the doorbell rings.

What about a luncheon Wednesday, for another example:

Melon-mint Cocktails

Piquant Crab Casserole   *Pineapple-lime Mold*

Savory Bread

Macaroon Pie   *Coffee*

And here's the way to schedule the cooking. Anytime in advance of Monday prepare the crab casserole and freeze. The week of your party, on Monday, prepare the melon cocktail and the pineapple mold. Tuesday prepare the bread and macaroon pie. Tuesday night defrost the casserole. Wednesday morning set the table. Whip a bowl of cream with which to top the pie and get your coffee maker set to go.

Forty minutes before you are ready to sit down, heat the crab casserole. Put the bread in the oven. And now await your guests.

This is all very well you say, but suppose guests arrive unexpectedly. How is it possible to relax and enjoy them, when you are frantically pulling together a meal? Well it isn't as easy as knowing two weeks in advance, but it can be done. Be prepared. Keep in your freezer or on your shelf a few already cooked or practically cooked meals. Then you can't be caught short!

Have a crab and mushroom casserole in your freezer. This dish needs only to be heated without defrosting to be served. Keep ingredients for shrimp Newburg, quick chow mein, or bachelor crabmeat handy and always have at least one dessert in the freezer: applesauce cake, brownies, ice cream. Have nuts, a jar of fudge sauce and coconut, etc., and you have the makings of a "Do-It-Yourself Sundae." Everyone will think you sent out to a local catering service!

Now let's tackle something on a large scale—carefully

thought out and prepared. For example a cocktail party on a Sunday afternoon.

Judiciously combine hot and cold hors d'oeuvres such as: biscuit hors d'oeuvres filled with bacon and tiny franks. These may be frozen and merely heated at party time. Also make and freeze cheese shorties and chafing-dish meatballs. Miniature pizzas may be put together and frozen, then defrosted and put under the broiler for a few minutes before serving.

In the dip department, try one bowl of red caviar dip and one of fruit of the sea. These may easily be prepared two days ahead.

For cold hors d'oeuvres—smoked salmon pinwheels which should be frozen and tiny cream puffs some filled with ham and some with cream cheese and Roquefort. The puffs may be frozen and merely reheated the day of your party to rejuvenate them. Pâté as well as the cheese filling may be made a day in advance and used to fill the puffs the morning of the party. One more beautiful as well as delicious addition to your table might be *Pâté en Gelée* which can be made the day before. The menu provides adequate quantity and selection for forty guests. It will also give you a colorful and interesting table. It would be divine to have a woman in the kitchen heating the hors d'oeuvres, etc., but you, yourself, can put them in the oven and still be the smiling, cheerful hostess.

We have tried to make each recipe as clear and concise as possible, so that the book can be used by a bride as well as an experienced cook. We hope that you will enjoy using it, as we certainly have enjoyed putting it together.

LOIS LEVINE and MARIAN BURROS

Helpful Information in Buying

THERE may have been a good reason for numbering cans (2½, 303, etc.) in the dim, dark past. But the reason is pretty obscure today. Especially since a No. 2½ can may contain anywhere from 28 to 30 ounces. (We're all for standardizing can sizes after we spend four hours in the grocery store trying to pin down some of these elusive numbers.)

Throughout the book we designate the size can required by the number of ounces it contains. But don't take it so literally that you will bypass a 1-pound 12-ounce can if the recipe calls for a 1-pound 13-ounce can. Maybe your store doesn't carry that size.

And for those who would like a short but not too accurate course in what the numbers mean, see the following chart.

CAN SIZE	APPROXIMATE WEIGHT	CUPFULS
6 oz	6 oz	¾
8 oz	8 oz	1
No. 1	10 to 12 oz	1¼ to 1½
No. 300	14 oz to 1 lb	1¾
No. 1½ or 303	1 lb to 17 oz	2
No. 2	1 lb 4 oz or 1 pint 2 fl. oz	2½
No. 2½	1 lb. 12 oz to 1 lb 14 oz	3½
No. 3 cylinder or 46 oz	3 lbs 3 oz or 1 quart 14 oz	5¾
No. 10	6 lbs 2 oz to 7 lbs 5 oz	12 to 13

I: Elegant but Easy
Hors D'oeuvres

Hot Hors D'oeuvres

Artichokes Ramaki

#1   *about 2 dozen*

Cook according to package directions
1 package frozen artichoke hearts (9 oz or about 24)
Drain and sprinkle with
Onion salt
Cut crosswise in half about
12 slices bacon

Wrap each half-slice around each artichoke heart. Refrigerate. To serve, broil 6 inches from heat about 8 minutes, turning once.

Bacon and Cheese Canapés

*#2   3 dozen

Mix together well

2 tablespoons butter   ½ teaspon paprika
8 oz cheddar cheese, grated   Salt
8 slices bacon, cooked and   Pepper
  finely chopped   2 eggs
½ teaspoon dry mustard

Refrigerate or freeze. When ready to serve, spread on toast
rounds and brown under broiler.

Biscuit Hors D'oeuvres

*#1   4 dozen

These have a catered look about them!

1 can refrigerator biscuits

Flatten each biscuit with palm of your hand. Cut each biscuit into quarters. In each quarter wrap

1 cocktail frankfurter with   sliver of cheese in slit

Refrigerate or freeze. To serve, bake at 450° F for about
5 minutes—until crisp.

Blintzes—Never Fail

*#2   *Old-fashioned recipe with exact proportions*

FILLING

Press

1 lb farmer cheese

through ricer or fine strainer

Mix with

1 egg   1 tablespoon soft butter
1 tablespoon sugar   Pinch salt

BATTER

Beat until light and foamy

2 eggs

Add

½ teaspoon salt	1 tablespoon melted butter
1 teaspoon sugar	1 cup flour, sifted with
1 cup water	¼ teaspoon baking powder

Beat until smooth. Drop this batter, 2 tablespoons at a time, onto greased (5-inch) frying pan, on medium heat. Tip pan so batter spreads thinly over entire pan. Pour off excess. Bake one side until top is dry and starts to blister. Turn out onto board. Fill with 1 tablespoon of filling. Roll and fold in sides. Refrigerate or freeze. When ready to serve, brush tops with melted butter. Bake at 400° F for ½ hour. Serve with sour cream, blueberries, etc.

Chafing-Dish Meatballs

*#2   50–60 meatballs

Probably the most popular hors d'oeuvres in the book.

Combine

2 lbs ground meat	1 large grated onion
1 slightly beaten egg	Salt to taste

Mix and shape into small balls. Drop into sauce of:

1 twelve-oz bottle chili sauce	Juice of 1 lemon
1 ten-oz jar grape jelly	

Simmer until brown. Refrigerate or freeze. To serve bring to room temperature. Reheat in chafing dish and serve with cocktail picks.

Cheddar Straws

*#1   6 dozen

Excellent with hot soup, aperitifs, or cold salads.

Sift together

1½ cups flour, sifted	¼ teaspoon dry mustard
1 teaspoon seasoned salt	

Cut in
½ cup butter
with pastry blender (preferably fingers), until it resembles
corn meal.

Sprinkle over mixture
3–3½ tablespoons water
Work until it forms a ball. Turn out on floured board;
role into rectangle ¼ inch thick. Sprinkle half the surface
with

⅓ cup shredded cheddar   1 teaspoon paprika
cheese

Fold plain half onto covered surface; pinch edges to seal.
Roll out to rectangle. Sprinkle with

⅓ cup cheddar cheese   1 teaspoon paprika

Repeat folding and sprinkling and folding. Roll into rec-
tangie. Cut into strips ½ inch wide and 3 inches long. Place
on ungreased cookie sheet. Bake at 425° F 10–12 minutes
or until slightly puffed and golden. Cool on wire racks.

Dip one end in
Paprika
Refrigerate or freeze. Refresh in 350° F oven before serving.

Cheese and Mushroom Canapés

*#2   2½ dozen

So easy and simply delicious!
Slice in tiny pieces
¼ lb mushrooms
Cook for a few minutes in
1 tablespoon butter
Mix mushrooms with

1 eight-oz package cream   Salt
cheese   Pepper
1 teaspoon minced onion   Add enough cream to soften
Toast on one side
Small rounds of bread

Spread the untoasted side with

Butter   **Mushroom mixture**

Refrigerate or freeze. When ready to serve, place under broiler until puffy and brown.

Cheese Shorties

*#3   *4 dozen*

Cream until fluffy

1 lb sharp cheddar cheese,   ½ lb butter
grated

Add

2 cups sifted flour   ½ teaspoon garlic salt

Make into rolls 1 inch in diameter and wrap in waxed paper. Chill or freeze. To serve, cut into ⅓-inch slices. Place on cookie sheet 1 inch apart. Bake at 400° F for 10 minutes.

Cheese Tarts, Miniature

*#1   *about 2 dozen*

Prepare

1 pie crust recipe

Roll out into rectangle same thickness as for pie crust. Cut into 2-inch squares. Press each square into 1-inch muffin cups.

Beat together thoroughly (with egg beater)

3 eggs   ¼ cup sour cream

Stir in

¼ lb finely grated Swiss   ¼ teaspoon poppy seeds
cheese   ⅛ teaspoon pepper

½ teaspoon grated onion

Place on bottom of each unbaked tart shell

Small piece crisp bacon

Fill tarts with cheese mixture. Refrigerate or freeze. When ready to serve bring to room temperature and bake tarts at 425° F for 5 minutes. Reduce oven to 325° F and bake 12 minutes longer, until brown.

Clam-Tomato Dip

*#2

Combine

2 six-oz cans tomato paste

2 ten and a half-oz cans minced clams, drained

1 teaspoon oregano

2 cloves garlic, cut up and browned in olive oil

2–4 teaspoons flour

Refrigerate or freeze. When ready to serve, heat and place in chafing dish. Serve with crackers as dippers.

Clams Casino

*#1   5 dozen

In water almost to cover, boil until they open

4 dozen cleaned little-neck clams

Remove meat from shells, saving

1 cup clam broth

Put clams through meat grinder with

2 hard-boiled eggs

Sauté until golden

6 large chopped onions

in

½ cup butter

Add clams and eggs to onions. Then add

1 cup bread crumbs

Mix to pasty consistency. Add enough

Clam juice to moisten

Stuff mixture in clam shells. Refrigerate or freeze. When ready to serve, cover each shell with

¼ strip of bacon

Refrigerate or freeze. To serve broil until bacon is brown, about 15 minutes.

Crabmeat Canapés

*#2   4 dozen

Whip together

6 oz cream cheese   ¼ cup heavy cream

Beat in
¼ cup mayonnaise
Add

1 teaspoon minced onion	½ clove garlic, mashed
½ teaspoon minced chives	Pinch salt

Marinate for 1 hour in

¼ cup lemon juice	½ lb crabmeat

Drain. Fold into sauce. Add

⅛ teaspoon Worcestershire sauce	2 drops hot pepper sauce

Refrigerate or freeze. To serve put on crackers and broil a few minutes, until lightly browned. Serve hot.

Crabmeat Crêpes

about 30 pieces

A true French delight. This is an authentic recipe and can be used for Crêpes Suzette, etc.

CRÊPES BATTER (*#7)

Put in a small bowl

4 heaping tablespoons flour	1 tablespoon vegetable oil
1 whole egg	3 tablespoons milk
1 egg yolk	

Stir with wire whisk until quite smooth.
Use enough from
1 cup milk
to make thin, creamlike consistency. Put in refrigerator for 3 or 4 hours. (It may be kept in refrigerator up to a week.) Remove and add enough of rest of milk to reduce to thin consistency again. Heat 6- or 7-inch frying pan; when very hot wipe out with piece of buttered waxed paper. Return to lowered heat. Cover bottom of pan with very thin layer of batter (pour off any excess). Cook until golden on one side; turn and cook on other side until golden. Stack them as they are cooked.

Spread crabmeat mixture on each crêpe. Roll like cylinder.

Cut into 3 pieces. Refrigerate or freeze. When ready to serve, defrost, heat in top of double boiler. Serve from chafing dish.

CRABMEAT FILLING (*#1)

Melt

2 tablespoons butter
  Remove from fire and stir in
2 tablespoons flour
  Stir in carefully

½ cup milk   ½ cup vegetable stock (can
                                be made with vegetable
                                bouillon cube)

Cook, stirring until smooth and boiling. Season with

Salt   Paprika

Sauté
6 shallots, finely chopped
in
3 tablespoons butter
  Add
½ lb crabmeat
  Add to sauce

2 beaten egg yolks   1 tablespoon chives, finely
1 tablespoon Madeira   chopped

Combination mixtures. Cool before filling crêpes.

Crabmeat Quiche

*#1   8 servings

Excellent! Lois' mother's best recipe.

CRUST

Sift together

1 cup flour   ⅛ teaspoon salt
1 tablespoon sugar   1 teaspoon baking powder
  Blend in
¼ lb butter

Mix thoroughly through hands until sugar is dissolved. If necessary add a few drops of water (not more than a teaspoon) to get a rolling consistency. Roll between waxed paper and line a 10-inch pie plate.

FILLING

Line unbaked pie shell with

½ lb Swiss cheese cut in slices ¼ inch thick

Cover with layer of

1 cup crabmeat	½ cup small cooked shrimp

Combine

1½ cups light cream	Dash of pepper
4 eggs, beaten	Dash of cayenne
1 tablespoon flour	¼ teaspoon nutmeg
½ teaspoon salt	

Stir in

2 tablespoons melted butter	2 tablespoons dry sherry

Beat well. Pour over seafood. Refrigerate or freeze. When ready to serve bring to room temperature and bake at 375° F for 40 minutes or until browned. Let stand for 20 minutes before serving.

Cream Puffs

*#2   50–60 miniature

One of the most elegant and impressive of hors d'oeuvres.

SHELLS

Heat oven to 400° F. Bring to boil in a 2-quart pot

1 cup water	½ cup butter

Reduce heat to low. Add

½ teaspoon salt	1 cup sifted all purpose flour

Cook, stirring vigorously until mixture leaves sides of pot and forms compact ball. Remove from heat. Cool slightly. Add one at a time, beating well after each addition

4 eggs

Drop by half-teaspoonfuls on ungreased cookie sheet and bake about 30 minutes until light and dry. When ready to use, cut off tops and fill with one of the following:

CREAM CHEESE AND HAM (*#3)

Combine

6 oz cream cheese   Catsup to moisten
1 three-oz can deviled ham

CREAM CHEESE AND ROQUEFORT (*#3)

Combine

3 oz cream cheese   Dry sherry to moisten
Roquefort to taste

SHRIMP SOUP (#1)

Let thaw completely
1 ten and one-quarter-oz can frozen shrimp soup
Add
2 heaping tablespoons sour cream

TONGUE (#1)

Melt
¼ lb butter
Add and stir until blended
½ cup flour
Gradually add
1½ cups milk
Cook over moderate heat until thickened; stirring constantly.
Stir in

1 cup cottage cheese   ½ teaspoon basil
¼ lb tongue, finely diced   ¼ teaspoon pepper
1 five-oz can water chest-   ½ teaspoon salt
nuts, diced

Fill 1-inch cream puffs with choice of mixtures. Replace tops. When ready to serve heat at 425° F.

Ham and Cheese Dip

*#2

Melt over low heat
1 lb cheddar cheese

Stir in

2 four and a half-oz cans deviled ham
2 teaspoons mustard
2 teaspoons Worcestershire sauce

Refrigerate or freeze. When ready to serve, heat and serve from chafing dish, with crackers as dippers.

Horseradish Meatballs

*#1   5 dozen

Mix together and shape into 1-inch balls

½ cup water
1 egg
½ cup bread crumbs
2 tablespoons prepared horseradish

1 cup water chestnuts, chopped
1 lb ground chuck

Bake 10 minutes in a shallow roasting pan at 350° F uncovered. When cool, cover with foil and freeze. When ready to serve bake for 15 minutes covered at 350° F then broil until brown. Serve with Marmalade Dip.

DIP

Combine and heat

⅓ cup orange marmalade
1 clove garlic, minced
¼ cup soy sauce

2 tablespoons lemon juice
⅓ cup water

Serve hot.

Meat-Filled Mushroom Caps

*#1   2 dozen

Remove stems from

2 dozen large mushrooms

Marinate caps for 1 hour in

½ cup soy sauce

Finely chop stems and mix with

½ lb ground beef
¼ cup minced green pepper
2 tablespoons bread crumbs
1 egg yolk

1 tablespoon minced onion
½ clove garlic
¼ teaspoon salt
¼ teaspoon pepper

Drain caps. Stuff with meat mixture mounded high. Brush tops with soy sauce. Broil 8–10 minutes. Refrigerate or freeze. When ready to serve, bring to room temperature and bake at 350° F for 8–10 minutes.

Olive-Cheese Nuggets

*#2   35 pieces

Shred

¼ lb sharp cheddar cheese

Blend with

¼ cup soft butter   ⅛ teaspoon salt
¾ cup sifted flour   ½ teaspoon paprika

Mix to form dough. Shape 1 teaspoon of dough around each of

35 small, stuffed green olives

Refrigerate or freeze. When ready to serve, bring to room temperature and place on ungreased baking sheet. Bake at 400° F for 12–15 minutes.

Oysters Rockefeller

*#1

Allow 4–6 oysters on half shell per person.

Place in each shell

1 teaspoon cooked chopped spinach

Place on top of that the oyster, then top each oyster with

Butter creamed with onion   Cooked bacon, minced
  juice   Dash of cayenne
Chopped parsley   Bread crumbs
Salt   Dot of Butter

Freeze or refrigerate. To serve return to room temperature and bake at 450° F to 500° F for 10 minutes or until oysters are plump and brown.

Sherley's Parmesan Puffs

#1

They disappear like soap bubbles.

Mix to a consistency of softened butter

Mayonnaise   Parmesan cheese, freshly
                              grated

Place in center of

Rounds of white bread, 1   About ⅛ teaspoon chopped
inch in diameter   onion

Cover bread round completely with

Mayonnaise-cheese mixture

Refrigerate if desired. To serve broil about 5–8 minutes
until puffed and brown. Serve immediately.

Pizzas, Miniature

*#2   3 dozen

You can never serve enough!

Spread

1 loaf party rye

with ingredients in order:

Tomato paste   Slice of Mozzarella cheese
Thin slice of salami   Dash of oregano

Refrigerate or freeze. When ready to serve, toast under
broiler until cheese is melted and beginning to brown.

Potato Pancakes, Miniature

*#1

Grate

4 very large potatoes

Drain off half of liquid. Add

2 beaten eggs   2 teaspoons onion, grated
1 teaspoon salt   ½ teaspoon baking powder
1 tablespoon flour

Mix well. Drop by teaspoonful onto hot greased skillet.
Brown well on both sides. Refrigerate or freeze. When ready

to serve, reheat in 450° F oven until very crispy. Serve with sour cream. To freeze or refrigerate, place between sheets of aluminum foil, or they will become soggy.

Ramaki

*#1   80–90 hors d'oeuvres

Cut in half
1 lb bacon, extra thin slices
Cut in quarters
2 five-oz cans water chestnuts
Cut in half
2 lbs chicken livers

Wrap piece of bacon around water chestnut and chicken liver. Fasten with toothpick. Marinate them for two hours in

1 cup soy sauce   ½ cup brown sugar

Drain and broil 3–4 minutes on each side, until bacon is not quite crisp. Remove toothpicks and freeze or refrigerate. When ready to serve, bring to room temperature and reheat in 400° F oven until bacon is really crisp.

Refrigerator Cheese Rolls

*#2   3 dozen

Grate
½ lb aged cheddar cheese
Add

3 tablespoons mayonnaise   2 teaspoons Worcestershire
1 tablespoon soft butter   sauce
                                  ½ teaspoon garlic salt

Remove crusts from
1 loaf sliced, fresh white bread

Roll thin. Spread mixture on bread. Roll up. Refrigerate or freeze. To serve return to room temperature; slice each roll in half. Broil until lightly browned.

Sesame Wafers

*#2   *about 3 dozen*

Cream

½ cup butter   4 oz cream cheese

Add

1 cup flour, sifted

Mix until smooth. Chill. Roll out on lightly floured board and cut into rounds—about 1 inch in diameter. Brush top of each with

Lightly beaten egg

Sprinkle with

Sesame seeds

Bake at 425° F 12–15 minutes. Refrigerate or freeze. Heat at 350° F to refresh at serving time.

Shrimp and Bacon

*#1   *60 hors d'oeuvres*

Marinate

3 lbs shrimp, raw, peeled and deveined

in

1 twelve-oz bottle chili sauce   2 cloves garlic

Wrap each shrimp in

Extra thin, sliced bacon, partially cooked

Freeze or refrigerate. When ready to serve, bring to room temperature and broil turning to brown evenly.

Shrimp and Cheese Nibblings
NIBBLINGS (#1)

2 lbs raw shrimp, shelled and   1 lb Swiss cheese, cubed
deveined   1 can pitted ripe olives

SAUCE (#3)

Sauté until crisp

4 slices bacon, cut in small pieces

Add and simmer to thickened mixture

4 tablespoons butter	⅛ teaspoon dried basil
1½ teaspoons garlic salt	⅛ teaspoon oregano
1 cup tomato paste	⅛ teaspoon marjoram
1 cup tomato juice	½ cup dry red wine
½ cup water	

Add

3 tablespoons lemon juice

Adjust seasonings. When ready to serve, heat sauce. Pour sauce into chafing dish, add shrimp, and cook until pink. Add cheese, olives. Serve with cocktail picks.

Spicy Sausage Balls

*#2   4 dozen

Mix together

1 lb spicy sausage meat	⅓ cup seasoned bread
1 slightly beaten egg	crumbs
	½ teaspoon sage

Shape into about 4 dozen balls. Brown them in skillet on all sides. Pour off grease.

Combine and add to meatballs

½ cup catsup and chili sauce combined	1 tablespoon vinegar
	1 tablespoon soy sauce
2 tablespoons brown sugar	

Cover and simmer 30 minutes. Refrigerate or freeze. When ready to serve, reheat, place in chafing dish, and serve with cocktail picks.

Sweet-and-Sour Franks

*#3   60–80 pieces

Mix

¾ cup prepared mustard   1 cup currant jelly

Place in top of double boiler.

Slice diagonally, ½ inch thick

2 lbs frankfurters

Add to sauce and cook for 5 minutes. Refrigerate or freeze. When ready to serve, place in chafing dish and heat. Serve with cocktail picks.

Swiss Fondue

#1

A rather hearty hors d'oeuvre and quite appropriate for a late supper. It has its own rules: Do not use a metal chafing dish. Spear cubes of bread and dip into the bubbling pot, stirring gently to keep the fondue blended. Lift out with twirling motion so you won't lose any of the cheese.

Cut into bite-sized pieces, giving each one a crusty side
1 one-lb loaf French bread
  Shred
1 lb imported Swiss cheese
  Mix together and set aside
2 tablespoons cornstarch   2 tablespoons kirsch
  Rub the chafing dish with cut surface of
1 clove garlic
  Put into the chafing dish shredded cheese and mixture of
¼ teaspoon salt   ⅛ teaspoon pepper
¼ teaspoon MSG
  Refrigerate. At serving time pour over this mixture
2 cups Neuchâtel wine
  When cheese is melted blend in
Cornstarch mixture
  Stir until bubbly. Guests start dipping when fondue bubbles.

Toasted Mushroom Rolls

*#3   3½ dozen
Guests vie to see who can eat the most.

PLAIN

Clean and chop fine
½ lb mushrooms

Sauté for five minutes in
¼ cup butter
Blend in

3 tablespoons flour   ¼ teaspoon MSG
¾ teaspoon salt

Stir in
1 cup light cream
Cook until thick. Add

2 teaspoons minced chives   1 teaspoon lemon juice

Cool. Remove crust from
1 family-sized loaf sliced, fresh white bread
Roll slices thin. Spread with mixture, roll up. Pack and
freeze, if desired. When ready to serve, defrost, cut each roll
in half, and toast on all sides in 400° F oven.

WITH LOBSTER

6 dozen

Add to Mushroom Mixture
1 lb lobster meat, minced
Follow directions for bread, using 2 regular-sized loaves.
Fill and roll. When ready to serve, slice in half, follow directions for plain rolls.

Cold Hors D'oeuvres

ABC Chip Dip

#3

Combine and mix lightly

⅓ cup toasted, chopped almonds

3 strips cooked bacon, crumbled

¾ cup mayonnaise

1½ cups sharp cheddar cheese, grated

1 tablespoon finely minced onion

¼ teaspoon salt

Serve with shredded wheat crackers.

Avocado and Bleu-Cheese Dip

#1   ½ cup

Peel and mash

1 avocado

Add to purée

¼ cup mashed bleu cheese

Stir in
1 tablespoon lemon juice
Season with
Salt   **Pepper**
Chill and serve with crackers.

Bleu-Cheese Almond Spread

#3   *2 cups*

Mash
4 oz bleu cheese
Blend in

½ cup crumbled soft cheddar cheese   **1 tablespoon Worcestershire sauce**

1 cup sour cream   **1 teaspoon paprika**

Add
½ cup toasted, slivered almonds
Spread on biscuits, toast.

Camembert Glacé

*#3   *12 servings*

Remove skin from
4 canned Camembert cheeses (four and a half oz total)
Mix with
½ lb butter
Pat back into shape and roll in
Bread crumbs

Place back in cans. Refrigerate or freeze. Serve at room temperature with toast or French bread slices.

Caviar Mold

#2   *fills 2-cup mold*

A little caviar can go a long way.
Blend until smooth

1 cup sour cream
1 cup creamed cottage
  cheese
1 clove garlic, crushed
¼ teaspoon seasoning salt
1 teaspoon Worcestershire
  sauce

A dash each of soy sauce,
  hot pepper sauce, celery
  salt, garlic salt, onion salt,
  black pepper, cayenne, paprika, and chili powder

Soften

1 envelope gelatin

in

¼ cup dry sherry

Place in pan and stir over low heat until granules disappear. Do not boil! Add gelatin to blender and whip. Pour
into lightly greased 1-pint mold and refrigerate until firm.
When ready to serve, unmold and top with
Caviar mixed with juice of ½ lemon
Note: If you use a heart-shaped mold, it will look like the
classic "coeur à la crème."

Cheddar-Cheese Balls

#1   *30 balls*
½ lb cheddar cheese
  (If you use the soft variety, roll into balls. If you use the
hard type, cut into balls with melon-ball cutter.)
  Chop separately until very fine
8 radishes   Sprigs of parsley
1 carrot

Roll about 10 balls in each kind of mixture.

Cheese-Almond Slices

*#2   40 pieces

Sauté until golden, then chop fine
1 cup blanched almonds
in 3 tablespoons butter

Cream together
3 oz cream cheese   ½ lb sharp cheddar cheese,
                             grated

Add almonds to cheese. Then add
1 pimiento, chopped   1 teaspoon Worcestershire
1 tablespoon lemon juice   sauce
1½ teaspoons salt   1 teaspoon grated onion
                             Dash paprika

Mix well. Shape into roll. Roll in
Chopped toasted almonds

Wrap in waxed paper. Refrigerate or freeze. To serve, defrost and cut into thin slices and serve with crackers.

Cheese Biscuits

#3   5 dozen

In a tin can these will keep 3 or 4 weeks.

Combine thoroughly until completely blended (use your fingers)
1 lb flour, sifted   1 lb finely grated, sharp
1 lb softened butter   cracker-barrel cheese

Divide into 5 or 6 portions and shape into cylinders about 1-inch in diameter. Chill for 2 hours and slice into ¼-inch slices and place on ungreased cookie sheet. Bake at 400° F 10–12 minutes. Remove immediately from baking sheet.

Chive-Anchovy Spread

#3   ½ cup

Mix

8 oz chive cream cheese   1 can rolled anchovies
1½ pimientos cut up fine

Refrigerate. Serve with crackers.

Chopped Liver

#2

Sauté

1 medium onion, finely chopped

in chicken fat or butter

Add

1 lb chicken livers

Sauté until just slightly pink inside. Season with salt and
pepper. Put through meat grinder, using small blade, with

1 small raw onion   1 hard-boiled egg

Add

Chicken fat

to make moist. (This mixture may be served on crisp
greens or placed in a decorative oiled mold. To remove, place
mold for a few seconds in hot water and invert.)

Serve with party rye or crackers.

Chive-Cheese Spread

#2

Mix

1 eight-oz package cottage   Sour cream to soften
  cheese with chives   1 teaspoon onion salt
1 four-oz package cream   1 teaspoon garlic salt
  cheese with chives   ½ teaspoon oregano
2 heaping tablespoons may-   Dash Worcestershire sauce
  onnaise

Refrigerate. Serve with crackers or party rye.

Clam Dip

#2

Drain, reserving juice
1 ten and a half-oz can minced clams

Combine clams with

6 oz cream cheese
2 teaspoons grated onion
¼ teaspoon hot pepper
sauce

⅛ teaspoon Worcestershire
sauce
¼ teaspoon lemon juice
½ teaspoon clam juice

Blend thoroughly. Chill. Serve with crackers or bread
rounds.

Cold-Cut Slices

#3

Cut ends off and remove soft crumbs from
3 very narrow, long French rolls

Brush insides with
Prepared mustard

Mash

6 slices liverwurst
12 slices garlic salami
2 hard-boiled eggs

2 tablespoons grated Swiss
cheese

Blend with

1 tablespoon each of
chopped parsley, chives,
grated onion

2 cloves garlic, minced

Add enough
Mayonnaise
to spread well and
2 teaspoons Worcestershire sauce

Fill rolls. Chill thoroughly. Slice thinly.

II : Elegant but Easy
Main Dishes

Meat

Beef and Onions—Chinese

#1   4 *servings*

Do not overcook any vegetables in Chinese cooking (or for that matter, ever!).

Heat

2 tablespoons oil (preferably peanut)

Sauté in oil very slightly

3 cups onion rings, thinly sliced

Add

2 tablespoons soy sauce   2 teaspoons dry sherry

½ teaspoon sugar

Continue to heat a few seconds. Remove from pan. Dredge

1 lb top round beefsteak, sliced very fine

in mixture of

4 teaspoons cornstarch	2 teaspoons dry sherry
2 tablespoons soy sauce	

Heat pan and add

4 tablespoons oil (preferably peanut)

Sauté beef until browned. Remove from fire. Add onions and refrigerate. When ready to serve reheat.

Beef Roulades

*#2   *4 servings*

A gourmet's delight!

BATTER

Mix and sift

1 cup flour, sifted	Dash salt
1 tablespoon sugar	

Beat and add to dry ingredients

3 eggs

Add and stir until smooth

1 cup milk

Add

2 tablespoons melted butter

Strain through fine sieve. Let stand at least three hours or overnight. Wipe heated 6-inch or 7-inch frying pan with buttered wax paper. Pour in about 3 tablespoons batter, pouring off any excess. When set and brown on underside, turn and brown other side. Repeat entire process making at least 8 very thin pancakes.

FILLING

Brown

¾ lb ground chuck, round, etc.	½ lb mushrooms, finely chopped
1 medium onion, finely chopped	

in

2 tablespoons butter

1 teaspoon
1 teaspoon oregano
¼ teaspoon rosemary

1 teaspoon dry mustard
2 garlic cloves, minced

bay leaf, crumbled
cheddar cheese,
crumbled
esan cheese,

Cover and simmer until cheese is almost all melted. Remove from heat. Spread beef mixture on pancakes. Fold in two sides and roll up. Place in greased baking dish. Sprinkle with

½ cup Parmesan cheese, shredded

Using
16 slices mozzarella cheese
place 2 on each roll. Sprinkle with

Paprika

Refrigerate or freeze. When ready to serve bring to room temperature, pour over

½ cup dry sherry

Bake at 350° F for 30 minutes. Mozzarella should be melted and browned.

#2

Blanquette de Veau

A French classic.
Simmer in deep covered pot for 1 hour or until tender   6 servings

2 lbs boned veal shoulder, cut in 1¼-inch pieces
with

1 quart boiling water
5 medium carrots, scraped and quartered
4 whole cloves, stuck in
1 small onion
1 bay leaf
⅛ teaspoon thyme
2 sprigs parsley
½ cup thinly sliced celery
4 peppercorns
1 tablespoon salt

Drain and reserve 3½ cups

ELEGANT BUT EASY

Melt
¼ cup butter
Add
15 small white onion...
Cover and simm... minutes
In same skille... ...hrooms
½ lb small, f...
in
½ c...

...onions to drained veal.

...p veal stock
Add veal and onions.
Melt
2 tablespoons butter
Remove from fire and add
¼ cup flour
Slowly add, constantly stirring
3 cups veal stock
Cook, stirring, over medium heat until thickened and boiling. Whisk slightly

2 egg yolks   **2 tablespoons lemon juice**

Slowly whisk in a little hot sauce. Then return all to rest of sauce. Combine veal and sauce.

Refrigerate or freeze. When ready to serve, heat but do not boil. Make a ring of rice or fluffy mashed potatoes and place veal in center. Sprinkle on
2 teaspoons or more snipped fresh dill

Boeuf Bourguignonne

*#2   *4–6 servings*

Combine in large casserole

2 lbs cubed beef (chuck, round steak, etc.)	**1 cup tomato sauce**
	1 clove garlic
3–4 carrots, cut up	**3 tablespoons quick cooking tapioca**
1 cup chopped celery	
2 onions, sliced	**1 tablespoon sugar**
2 cups canned tomatoes	**½ cup red Burgundy**

Cook at 250° F for 5 hours. During last hour add

1 cup sliced water chestnuts   2 one-lb cans small Irish po-
1 six-oz can mushrooms   tatoes

After four hours of cooking, freeze, if desired. To serve, defrost and cook at 250° F for 1 hour, adding water chestnuts, mushrooms, and potatoes.

Carbonnade of Beef

#2   10 *servings*

Overnight marinate

1½ cups dried prunes   1½ cups dried apricots

in

1½ cups beer   ½ teaspoon ground ginger

Sprinkle with salt and allow to stand 1 hour

6 lb boneless fresh brisket of beef

In large Dutch oven or heavy pot brown beef on all sides in own fat. Add and brown

2 onions, sliced

Add

¼ cup water

Simmer 1 hour. Cool. Remove meat from stock and slice. Skim fat off meat. Return meat to stock with

½ teaspoon cinnamon   ⅓ cup honey
Dash pepper   ½ cup brown sugar

Simmer 1 hour, covered. Add

10 medium potatoes, thinly   1½ cups dried prunes
   sliced   1½ cups dried apricots

Pour in marinade. Simmer, covered, about 30 minutes more. Refrigerate. When ready to serve, reheat. Place meat slices down middle of platter and arrange potatoes and fruit around edges.

Chili Con Carne

*#2   4 *servings*

Brown in small amount

Cooking oil   2 onions, chopped

Add and brown
1½ lbs ground chuck
Add

1 ten and a half-oz can tomato soup	½ of 1 lb can kidney beans, mashed
1 lb can tomatoes	

Simmer 1 hour.
Add

Rest of kidney beans, whole   1 teaspoon chili powder

Simmer 5 minutes more. Refrigerate or freeze. When ready to serve, reheat and serve on spaghetti or macaroni shells.

Chinese Beef

#1   *6 servings*

Cut into thin strips across the grain
1 flank steak
Cut up and set aside

2 fresh tomatoes, quartered	2 green peppers, ribs and seeds removed, cut in chunks

Heat in skillet
2 tablespoons salad oil
Add beef and brown on all sides with

1 clove garlic	Dash pepper
1 teaspoon salt	¼ teaspoon ground ginger

Cover tightly and cook slowly for 5 minutes. Toss in

Tomatoes	1 one lb can bean sprouts
Peppers	

Bring to a boil, cover and cook briskly for 5 minutes.
Make a paste of

1 tablespoon cornstarch	¼ cup water

Add to beef mixture and cook until sauce thickens, about 5 minutes. Stir occasionally. When ready to serve, reheat.

Chinese Spareribs

*#1   4 servings

In Chinese style . . .

Mash or grind to fine pulp

6 cloves garlic

Mix with

1 tablespoon salt

Mix above ingredients with

1 cup honey   2 cups chicken stock (made
½ cup soy sauce   with 2 bouillon cubes)
                               ½ cup catsup

Marinate overnight in sauce

4 lbs spareribs, cut into small pieces

Baste and turn occasionally. Refrigerate or freeze. When
ready to serve, bring to room temperature, put spareribs and
marinade in roasting pan and bake at 450° F for 10 minutes,
reduce heat and bake at 325° F for 60 to 80 minutes. Baste
frequently. Serve with marinade and rice.

Churrasco Roast

#2   8 to 10 servings

In large shallow roasting pan place

6–8 lb rolled boneless sirloin tip or rump roast

Combine and pour following mixture over roast.

2 tablespoons minced onion   ½ cup olive or salad oil
2 teaspoons thyme   1 cup wine vinegar
1 teaspoon marjoram   3 tablespoons lemon juice
1 bay leaf crushed   1 clove garlic, minced

Stand at room temperature at least 2 hours, turning beef
and spooning marinade over occasionally. Then refrigerate
at least overnight. Remove meat from marinade and place
on spit; outdoors, 15 minutes to the pound for rare; indoors,
15–18 minutes to the pound for rare. Slice thinly. May be
served with juices spooned over.

Daube de Boeuf Provençale

#1   *6–8 servings*

Very French.

Daube indicates a style of braising utilizing red or white wine.

Cut into 1½-inch pieces

4 lbs top round beef

Season with

Thyme   Salt and pepper
Bay leaf

Marinate for 2 hours in mixture of

1 bottle dry white wine   3 tablespoons olive oil

Drain the beef and place in deep casserole.

Spread the pieces of beef in layers, alternating with

12 fresh diced bacon rinds   4 tomatoes, chopped
8 carrots, sliced   3 cloves garlic, crushed
2 onions, chopped   16 pitted black olives
1 cup mushrooms, chopped

Place, in center of these ingredients, a

"Bouquet garni" (parsley, thyme, bay leaf tied in piece of
cheesecloth)

Add

1 orange peel

Pour the marinating liquor over all. Refrigerate if desired.
To serve, cook at 275° F for 5 hours or to desired degree of
doneness. Before serving remove "bouquet garni."

Fondue Bourguignonne

This dish really needs a separate chapter. There is an
ordered ritual for eating it and prescribed utensils and pots
for cooking it. But there are many substitute utensils that
work well, too, and do not detract from the fun or intimacy
of this type of dinner.

Each guest will need a plate and 2 forks, one with a long
shaft. A casserole or chafing dish is filled with salad oil and

kept piping hot over an alcohol flame. The group must be small enough to be within easy reach of the oil—not more than 8 people per pot.

A bowl of bite-sized pieces of very tender beef, such as **sirloin** or **tenderloin** (8 oz per person), and a variety of sauces are the ingredients.

The guest, using the long handled fork, takes a piece of beef, places it in the boiling oil, where it sizzles delightfully, and cooks it until it is done as much as he desires. He transfers it to his own place, salts and peppers it and then, using the second fork, dips it in one of the sauces offered, such as those below.

*#3 ½ cup

GARLIC BUTTER

Combine and beat with fork

½ cup softened butter   Salt and pepper to taste
3 cloves garlic, minced

Refrigerate or freeze. Have at room temperature when serving.

*#3 1½ cups

TOMATO STEAK SAUCE

In saucepan combine all ingredients

1 eight-oz can tomato sauce   2 tablespoons brown sugar
⅓ cup **bottled** steak sauce   2 tablespoons salad oil

Refrigerate or freeze. When ready to serve, bring to boil. Serve hot.

#3 1¼ cups

HORSERADISH SAUCE

Combine

1 cup sour cream   ¼ teaspoon salt
3 tablespoons white horse-   Dash paprika
radish

Refrigerate until serving time.

Hollandaise, Béarnaise, curry flavored mayonnaise are additional sauces.

Some or all of the following condiments may also be served:

Chutney, slivered almonds, grated coconut, spiced pineapple tidbits, parsley, small white onions, pickled beets, pickle relish, cocktail onions, olives, salted peanuts, and chives.

Gourmet Leg of Lamb

#1   6 servings

Roast

Leg of lamb

at 300 degrees, 30 to 35 minutes to the pound, basting frequently with the following sauce.

Beat well

2 tablespoons chili sauce
1½ tablespoons Worcestershire sauce
1½ tablespoons vinegar

3 tablespoons olive oil
Dash of each: salt, pepper, thyme, and powdered bay leaf

Stir in

1 ten and a half-oz can beef bouillon

2 tablespoons minced onion
1 clove garlic

Lamb may be wrapped in aluminum foil and reheated when ready to serve.

Ham-and-Tongue Mousse

#2   6 servings

Lovely to look at, delightful to eat.

Sauté for 2 to 3 minutes

3 tablespoons finely chopped shallots

in

1 tablespoon butter

Dissolve

2 envelopes unflavored gelatin

in

⅓ cup dry white wine

Add to dissolved gelatin

2 cups hot chicken stock

Reserve enough clear liquid to cover bottom of 1½-quart mold. Pour into mold and chill until sticky-firm.

Decorate with

Halved, pitted black olives

To remaining gelatin mixture add shallots.

Cube 2⅓ cups cooked smoked ham. Place in blender

½ cup hot liquid   ⅔ cup ham (from 2⅓ cups)

Blend thoroughly. Pour mixture into bowl. Repeat process until all liquid and all ham are blended.

Into ham mixture stir

2 tablespoons brandy   Salt and freshly ground pep-
1½ tablespoons tomato   per to taste
  paste

Cool mixture. When it starts to thicken add

½ cup finely diced, cooked   1½ tablespoons fresh dill,
  tongue   minced (or 1 teaspoon
                                     dried dill)
                                ¾ cup heavy cream, whipped

Spoon into mold and chill overnight. To serve, unmold on bed of greens and serve with Sour Cream Horseradish Sauce.

SOUR CREAM HORSERADISH SAUCE

#3   1 cup

Combine and chill until serving time

1 cup sour cream   1 teaspoon prepared mustard
2 tablespoons prepared white
  horseradish

Hamburger Kebob

#1   6 servings

Excellent for cookouts.

Combine

1¾ lbs ground chuck   Salt
2 teaspoons grated onion   Pepper
Dash Worcestershire sauce

Make into walnut-sized balls and broil until brown. Broil

6 strips bacon, cut in half

Sauté

12 mushroom caps   **6 chicken livers, cut in half**

in

2 tablespoons butter

Thread on 6 skewers in this order:

Hamburger	**Folded bacon**
Mushroom cap	**Chicken liver**

End with meat. Dip all in

Melted butter

Broil either outside or inside turning frequently.

Lamb Curry

*#1   *6–8 servings*

Sauté until golden

2 cloves garlic   **4 onions, sliced**

in

¾ cup butter

Add

3 lbs raw cubed lamb, dredged in flour

Sauté for 10 minutes. Stir. Add

3 tablespoons curry powder   **3 tart apples, peeled and chopped**

Simmer for 5 minutes. Stir. Add

1 cup walnuts, chopped	**4 tablespoons coconut**
2 lemons, sliced	**4 tablespoons brown sugar**
4 tablespoons raisins	**1 tablespoon salt**

Pour over all

3 cups water

Bring to boil. Reduce heat, simmer for 1 hour. When ready to serve, reheat.

Indian Pilaf

*#1 *4 servings*

Unusual use of leftover meat.
Bring to a boil

1 cup rice   1 teaspoon curry powder
2½ cups chicken stock
Cook slowly until liquid is absorbed.
Sauté until golden
4 sliced onions
Add

½ cup white raisins   2 small bay leaves, crushed
4 tablespoons salted   ½ teaspoon nutmeg
  almonds, chopped   Pepper
½ teaspoon cinnamon
Mix with rice. Add
2 cups cooked chicken or lamb
cut in julienne strips. Freeze or refrigerate. When ready to
serve, reheat.

Italian Grill

#1 *6 servings*

For cookouts.
Cut into 1½-inch cubes
3 lbs boneless veal
Marinate meat for 2 hours in mixture of

1 cup Italian dressing   1 teaspoon oregano
Scrub, cube, and parboil
1 lb zucchini
Cut into squares
3 red peppers
Cut into cubes
½ lb sharp cheddar
Wrap each cheese cube with
½ slice bacon
Alternately thread ingredients on skewers. Refrigerate.
Outdoors or indoors broil 2–3 inches from heat, about 20
minutes.

Lasagna
*#3   6–8 *servings*

If you like Italian food, don't miss this!

Simmer uncovered

1 one-lb twelve-oz can peeled tomatoes	1½ teaspoons oregano
	⅛ teaspoon pepper
2 eight-oz cans tomato sauce	1 teaspoon onion salt
1 teaspoon salt	

In skillet sauté until light brown

1 cup minced onions   1 clove garlic, minced

in

3 tablespoons olive or salad oil

Add

1 lb ground chuck or round   1 teaspoon salt
1 teaspoon MSG

Cook until meat is light brown. Add to tomato sauce and simmer 2½ hours or until thickened.

Cook according to package directions

1 one-lb box lasagna noodles

Drain and separate noodles on paper.

For layering:

1 lb ricotta cheese   1 eight-oz package mozza-
1 cup Parmesan cheese,   rella cheese, thinly sliced
  grated

Cover bottom of casserole with several spoonfuls of sauce. Top with criss-cross layer of noodles, then ricotta, mozzarella, and Parmesan. Repeat, ending with sauce and topping with mozzarella. Refrigerate or freeze. When ready to serve, bring to room temperature and bake at 350° F for 50 minutes.

Meat Sauce for Spaghetti
*#3   4 *servings*

Brown slowly in saucepan

1 lb ground chuck   ½ medium onion, chopped
1 tablespoon olive oil   1 teaspoon parsley
1 garlic clove, crushed

Add

1 one-lb can tomatoes   ½ teaspoon basil
2 six-oz cans tomato paste   1 teaspoon oregano
⅛ teaspoon pepper

Cover pan and simmer 1 hour. Add

1 tablespoon butter

When ready to serve, reheat and serve over

1 lb spaghetti

Pastisto

*#2   6 servings

Cook, then drain

1 lb elbow macaroni

Sauté for 3 minutes

2 onions chopped   1 lb ground chuck
in
¼ lb melted butter

Add

1 tomato peeled and   Salt
chopped   Pepper

Cook until meat is brown and tender. Blend in

½ cup grated American cheese

In buttered casserole place half of macaroni, cover with
meat. Top with rest of macaroni. Top with meat. In small
saucepan, melt

2 tablespoons butter

Remove from heat and blend in

2 tablespoons flour

Slowly blend in, stirring

1 cup milk

Add

¼ cup grated American   1 beaten egg
cheese

Return to low heat and cook until thickened.

Pour over macaroni. Refrigerate or freeze. When ready to
serve bring to room temperature and bake at 350° F for 40
minutes.

Pot Roast

*#1   8 servings

Excellent flavor.

Cut small and fry until golden

6 medium onions

in

2 tablespoons shortening

Set onions aside. In heavy pot brown on all sides

6 lbs brisket of beef

Sprinkle with

Salt   Pepper

Cover tightly and simmer slowly for 2½ hours. Then add

Onions	2 tablespoons brown sugar
1 cup catsup	1 ten and a half-oz can to-
2 tablespoons lemon juice	mato soup

If you wish, freeze at this point. When ready to serve, defrost and cook another ½ hour. Reheat at serving time. Excellent with potato pancakes (p. 23).

Rolled Cabbage

*#3   4–6 servings

Boil until soft, 15–30 minutes

1 medium head cabbage

Cool and remove leaves carefully. This is best accomplished by first removing core. Combine and mix thoroughly

| 1 lb ground chuck | 1 medium onion finely |
| | chopped |

Place small amount of meat in leaf (depending on size of leaf) and roll.

In pot place cabbage rolls with

1 sliced onion	Lemon juice
1 one-lb can whole tomatoes	Raisins
Brown sugar	Salt or citric acid salt

(The amount of sugar and lemon varies so greatly depending on individual taste that frequent tasting is neces-

sary and no set proportions can be given.) Simmer, covered,
very slowly for 2 hours. Refrigerate or freeze. When ready
to serve, return to room temperature, place in shallow pan
in oven for ½ hour at 350° F. Baste often and brown well.
Adjust seasoning if necessary.

Saltimbocca

*#2   *4 servings*

An elegant Italian dish.
Start with

8 thin slices prosciutto ham	2 lbs thin veal steak cut in 8 pieces, and flattened to ⅛ inch

Top each piece of veal in the following order

Slice of mozzarella	Pinch ground sage
Slice of prosciutto	Pinch salt
1 teaspoon melted butter	1 teaspoon snipped parsley
Pinch freshly ground pepper	Second piece of veal

Pinch edges of top and bottom veal slice together. Dip in
flour to coat both sides. In large skillet, heat

4 tablespoons butter	4 tablespoons olive oil

Sauté Saltimbocca on both sides, until lightly brown.
Refrigerate or freeze until ready to serve. To serve bring to
room temperature, pour on
⅓ cup sherry
Simmer about 20 minutes or until tender. May be served
from chafing dish.

Satés

*#1   *6 servings*

MARINADE
Mash thoroughly and combine

6 grated Brazil nuts	1 tablespoon salt
2 tablespoons coriander seeds	1 hot red pepper, seeded and chopped
2 garlic cloves, minced	

Add to above mixture

8 onions grated
2 tablespoons brown sugar
4 tablespoons soy sauce

1 teaspoon ground black
pepper
3 tablespoons lemon juice

Marinate overnight in this mixture

2 lbs lean pork cubes

Refrigerate or freeze. When ready to serve bring to room temperature and broil on both sides.

Shish Kebobs

*#1   6 servings

Excellent for outdoor cookery, too.

Cut up into 1-inch cubes

½ of leg of lamb (use 3–4 lbs lamb)

Marinate for at least 6 hours in mixture of

6 tablespoons lemon juice
4 tablespoons olive oil
2 tablespoons grated onion
½ teaspoon cayenne

1 teaspoon ginger
1 clove garlic, mashed
2 teaspoons curry powder
1 tablespoon salt

The marinated meat may be frozen or refrigerated.
When ready to serve thread alternately on 6 skewers

Meat
18 mushroom caps
24–30 canned pineapple
chunks

2 green peppers, cut into
eighths

Broil for 45 minutes.

Spaghetti Superb

*#1   6 servings

Lightly brown

1 lb ground chuck
½ cup chopped onion
in
2 tablespoons shortening

¼ cup chopped green pep-
per

Stir occasionally. Add and heat

1 ten and a half-oz can cream of mushroom soup

1 ten and a half-oz can tomato soup

1 soup can water

1 clove garlic, minced

½ lb spaghetti, cooked and drained

½ cup shredded sharp cheese

Place in 3 quart casserole. Top with

½ cup shredded sharp cheese

Refrigerate or freeze. To serve bake at 350° F for 30 minutes.

Steak Diane

4 servings

For husbands to make in front of the company!

In a large heavy skillet melt

4 tablespoons butter

Sauté in it until golden

2 tablespoons shallots

Put in skillet

4 individual portions sirloin steak (about 2 lbs) pounded and trimmed

Sear them quickly on both sides. Add

2 tablespoons heated brandy

Flame the brandy and when it dies down add

4 tablespoons dry sherry

Chopped chives

Minced parsley

Worcestershire sauce

Steak sauce

2 tablespoons butter

Mix well. Sprinkle steaks with

Salt and freshly ground pepper

Continued to sauté until done. Because the steaks are so thin they will take very little time to cook.

Stuffed Sweet Peppers

6 servings

*#1

Cut in half, lengthwise

3 large green peppers

Remove seeds and scald in hot water 4–5 minutes. Drain and fill with following mixture:

In large skillet brown

1 lb ground veal   ½ onion, chopped

in

2 tablespoons butter
    Add

1 cup boiled rice   2 chopped hard-boiled eggs
2 scalded, peeled tomatoes,   2 tablespoons sour cream
    chopped
    Season to taste with
Salt and pepper
    Stuff pepper halves and place in baking dish.
    Sprinkle with
Grated American cheese
    Refrigerate or freeze. When ready to serve return to room temperature and bake at 350° F for ½ hour.

Sweet-and-Sour Tongue

*#1   4 servings
    Also excellent for using left-over tongue.
    Cook

6 slices bacon
    Remove from pan. Sauté

2 sliced onions in bacon drippings
    Blend in

2–3 tablespoons flour
    Slowly add

4 cups beef stock (made with 4 bouillon cubes and 4 cups
    of water)
    Let thicken and add

4 tablespoons honey   4 tablespoons vinegar
1 cup raisins   4 cups tongue, julienned
    Refrigerate or freeze. When ready to serve, bring to room temperature and simmer for 15 minutes. Garnish with bacon.

Teriyaki

*#1   6 servings

Nice outside, too.
Combine

1 tablespoon finely chopped
fresh ginger or 2 teaspoons
powdered

2 cloves garlic, chopped fine

1 medium onion, chopped
fine

2 tablespoons sugar

½ cup soy sauce

1 cup water

Pour this mixture over

2 lbs sirloin steak cut into strips ¼ inch thick

Marinate overnight. Refrigerate or freeze. When ready to
serve bring to room temperature, place meat on shallow pan
and broil 3–5 minutes on each side.

Veal and Water Chestnuts

*#2   6 servings

Brown

2 lbs boneless veal, cut for stew

in

4 tablespoons butter

Add

1 clove garlic, crushed

1 medium onion, grated

Transfer meat to covered casserole. In same frying pan
sauté

1 lb fresh mushrooms, sliced

Add mushrooms to meat.

Add to casserole

½ cup beef bouillon

⅛ teaspoon nutmeg

1 bay leaf

1 twelve-oz can water chestnuts, sliced

Stir and cover. Cook at 375° F until tender, about 1½
hours.

Then add

1 cup heavy cream

Cook uncovered for 15 minutes more. Sprinkle with
1 tablespoon parsley
Refrigerate or freeze. When ready to serve bring to room
temperature and reheat.

Veal Parmesan

*#3   6–8 servings

SAUCE

Heat in saucepan
¼ cup olive oil
Add and brown lightly

| ½ cup chopped onion | 1 lb ground chuck |

Add

2 one-lb twelve-oz cans to-   1 tablespoon salt
matoes (sieved to discard   1 bay leaf
seeds)   1 six-oz can tomato paste
Simmer, covered, 2½–3 hours, until thickened.

VEAL (*#1)

Dip
2 lbs veal cutlets (Italian style—very thin)
into mixture of

Seasoned bread crumbs   Parmesan cheese, grated

then into mixture of

3 eggs, well beaten   Salt and pepper

then into crumbs again. Brown slices on each side in
⅓ cup olive oil
Alternate in casserole layers of

Cutlets   2 eight-oz packages mozza-
Tomato-meat sauce   rella cheese, sliced

Top with sauce. Refrigerate or freeze. When ready to serve
return to room temperature, bake at 350° F for 20 minutes
or until cheese is melted and browned.

Poultry

Baked Imperial Chicken with Cumberland Sauce

*#2   *6–8 servings*

Mix

½ cup grated Parmesan
   cheese

2 cups seasoned bread
   crumbs

3 tablespoons sesame seeds

Cut up into serving pieces

2 two and a half- to three-lb broilers or fryers

Dip pieces in

½ cup melted butter

then in

Crumb mixture

Freeze or refrigerate. When ready to serve bring to room temperature, place in shallow pan. Dot with

Butter

Bake one hour at 350° F. Serve with Cumberland Sauce if desired.

SAUCE

Combine and simmer until smooth

1 cup red currant jelly	4 tablespoons dry sherry
1 six-oz can frozen orange juice concentrate, defrosted	1 teaspoon dry mustard
	⅛ teaspoon ground ginger
	¼ teaspoon hot pepper sauce

Breezy Barbecued Chicken

*#2   6 servings

This took a prize at the Delmarva Chicken Contest!

Marinate in mixture below

2 two and a half-lb broilers, quartered
  Combine

1 cup salad oil	1 teaspoon dry mustard
⅓ cup wine vinegar	1 tablespoon Worcestershire sauce
3 tablespoons sugar	
3 tablespoons catsup	1 clove garlic, minced
1 tablespoon grated onion	Dash hot pepper sauce
1½ teaspoons salt	

Marinate chicken pieces in this sauce overnight. Refrigerate or freeze. To serve, return to room temperature. For outdoors, broil over gray charcoal fire, 12 inches from coals, 20 minutes each side, turning frequently and basting often. If there is any marinade left, serve it hot with chicken. Indoors, broil as far from heat source as possible, basting and turning often.

Chicken and Grapes

#1   6 servings

So-o-o elegant but easy!

In large skillet heat

6 tablespoons butter

In it brown
2 two and a half-lb fryers, cut into pieces, salted and peppered
Transfer chicken to casserole. In same frying pan brown
2 tablespoons finely chopped onion
Add and heat
1 cup dry white wine
Pour over chickens and bake covered for 30 minutes. Refrigerate.
Bring to room temperature; when ready to serve add
2 cups seedless grapes
Bake the chicken ½ hour more at 350° F.

Chicken Breast Maryland

*#1   *4–6 servings*
*The real name of this lovely dish might scare you away—
Suprêmes de Volaille Virginie—so we translated it, and
since Marian lives in Maryland Virginie changed too.*
Skin and bone (or have your butcher do so)
6 whole chicken breasts
Put each breast between 2 sheets of waxed paper and pound
flat with cleaver or rolling pin.
Between the halves of each breast place
1 thin slice well-seasoned ham (shaped to fit breast)
that has been dipped in
4 lightly beaten eggs
Fold over half of breast and press closed at edges. Egg
helps to seal it. Dip chicken–ham piece in eggs. Then dip in
Seasoned bread crumbs
Melt in large skillet
¼ lb plus 2 tablespoons butter
Place chicken breasts in skillet and sauté for 15 minutes,
browning on both sides. At this point you may refrigerate
or freeze the breasts in a baking dish with the butter sauce
poured over them. When ready to serve bring to room temperature and bake for 20 minutes or until heated through at
350° F.

Chicken Breasts Piquant

*#1   *4 servings*

An unusual tang.
Combine

1½ cups rosé or dry red wine   2 cloves garlic, sliced
½ cup soy sauce   2 teaspoons ground ginger
½ cup salad oil   ½ teaspoon oregano
4 tablespoons water   2 tablespoons brown sugar
Arrange in baking dish
4 whole chicken breasts
Pour mixture over top. Refrigerate or freeze. When ready
to serve return to room temperature, cover and bake at 375° F
about 1 hour. Serve with rice. (This may also be made with
cut-up whole chicken.)

Chicken Cacciatore

*#2   *4–6 servings*

Cut into individual pieces
2½–3-lb broiler, fryer, or roaster
Sauté pieces until golden brown in
¼ cup or more olive or salad oil
Add

1 large onion, chopped   ¼ teaspoon pepper
1 one-lb can whole tomatoes   ½ bay leaf
1 eight-oz can tomato sauce   ⅛ teaspoon thyme
½ cup dry white wine   ¼ teaspoon marjoram
1 teaspoon salt   1 clove garlic, cut up
Cover chicken. Simmer for 1 hour, or until tender.
Refrigerate or freeze. When ready to serve, return to room
temperature, reheat and serve with spaghetti.

Chicken Chinoise

*#1   *6 servings*

Great luncheon casserole.
Cook and then cool in the stock
1 five-pound chicken (or 2 two and a half-lb chickens)

Strain and cool the stock. Cook and drain
½ pound green noodles
Parboil and drain well
4–6 carrots, slivered
Melt
4 tablespoons butter
Stir in
4 tablespoons flour
Add and cook until thick

2 cups chicken stock   **2 tablespoons cream**
Season to taste with
Salt and pepper
Add

Chicken meat, diced   **8 canned water chestnuts,**
Carrots   **sliced**

Line a baking dish with noodles. Pour in chicken mixture.
Top with
½ cup prepared packaged stuffing mix
Dot with
Butter
Refrigerate or freeze. When ready to serve bring to room
temperature and bake at 400° F for 30 minutes or until hot
and bubbling.

Chicken Curry in Pineapple Shells

#1   *6 servings*
*Impressive looking and delicious. . . . Not too hot to the
taste!*
Melt
¼ cup shortening
Add

2 small chopped onions   **1 stalk celery**
1 clove garlic, minced   **1 tart apple, diced**

Cook for 8 minutes, occasionally stirring. Stir in

¼ cup flour   **1 teaspoon salt**
2 teaspoons curry powder   **½ teaspoon dry mustard**

Cook for 2 minutes, stirring. Add
1 bay leaf
Gradually add
2 cups chicken stock
Stir until sauce thickens. Cook for 30 minutes longer over low heat. Add

½ cup light cream
2 tablespoons chutney

1 cup diced fresh pineapple (or crushed canned pineapple, drained, if fresh is not available)

Add
3 cups cooked chicken, diced
Cool.
Cut
3 small pineapples*
in half lengthwise. Cut out fruit, leaving ½-inch thick shell. Two or 3 hours before serving fill shells with mixture.
Top with
Shredded coconut
When ready to serve, arrange on baking dish and bake at 350° F for 20–30 minutes or until heated thoroughly.

Chicken Divan

*#1   6 servings

It is divine chicken, too.
Place in bottom of 3 quart casserole
2 ten-oz packages frozen broccoli, cooked
Place on top of broccoli
2 cups of chicken, sliced and cooked
In small saucepan melt
6 tablespoons butter
Blend in
6 tablespoons flour

* If fresh pineapple is not in season, serve filling from casserole over Coconut Rice. See Vegetables, p. 125.

Add gradually, and cook stirring until thick
3 cups chicken stock
Add to sauce

½ cup heavy cream
½ teaspoon Worcestershire
sauce
1 cup shredded Parmesan
cheese

4 teaspoons prepared mustard
2 tablespoons minced onion
2 tablespoons dry sherry
Salt and pepper to taste

Stir over low heat until cheese is melted. Pour sauce over meat and broccoli. Refrigerate or freeze. When ready to serve, return to room temperature; bake at 400° F for 25–30 minutes. Before bringing to table dash sherry generously over all.

Chicken Florentine

*#1   6 servings

Cook according to package directions
2 ten-oz packages frozen chopped spinach
Drain well. Then melt
1 tablespoon butter
Cook in it and stir constantly
1 clove garlic, mashed   Dash basil
Dash marjoram
Add and mix well
1 tablespoon flour
Add
⅓ cup medium or heavy   Spinach
cream
Place mixture on bottom of casserole. Cover with
Meat from 1 five-lb stewed chicken
Melt
3 tablespoons butter
Add and blend well
3 tablespoons flour

Stir in and cook until thickened.

¾ cup cream   Salt and pepper to taste
¾ cup chicken stock

Pour sauce over chicken. Cover with

1 cup grated Parmesan cheese

Refrigerate or freeze. When ready to serve, return to room temperature; bake at 400° F for 20 minutes or until cheese is bubbling.

Chicken Gloriosa

#2   8 servings

Over

2 three-lb chickens, cut up
squeeze

2 tablespoons lime or lemon   Salt and pepper
    juice

Let chickens stand for 2 hours.

Drain, reserving juice and sauté chickens in

1 cup oil   2 cloves garlic, crushed

When thoroughly browned, remove chicken to shallow baking dish (9 x 13) and in same oil fry

6 slices very ripe fresh pine-   ½ cup fine bread crumbs
    apple, cut in wedges
    Add

Leftover citrus juices   Salt and pepper to taste
1 scant teaspoon hot pepper   ½ cup white raisins
    sauce   4 tablespoons tomato paste
2 pinches saffron   ½ cup sherry

Pour sauce over chicken. Garnish with

1 eleven-oz can mandarin oranges

When ready to serve, cover with foil and bake at 350° F for 1 hour. Serve on

Saffron rice, cooked according to package directions

Chicken in Sour Cream

*#1   4 *servings*

Brown

1 large broiler, quartered

in

3 tablespoons butter

In same pan, brown

1 large onion, chopped

Add

½ cup dry white wine   Pinch basil
2–3 sprigs parsley   Pinch thyme

Sprinkle with salt and pepper. Cover and simmer for 1 hour. During last ½ hour add

½ lb whole mushrooms

Refrigerate or freeze. When ready to serve, bring to room temperature; reheat. Just before serving stir in

½ pint sour cream

Heat but do not boil.

Chicken Italienne

*#1   6 *servings*

Shake

6 breasts of chicken, halved

or

2 broilers, quartered

in bag containing

Flour   Salt

Sauté until golden in

4 tablespoons butter or chicken fat

Place in large casserole.

In same pan used to sauté chicken, brown

4–5 onions, sliced

in

2 tablespoons fat or butter

Add

6–8 stalks celery, cut up	2 ten and a half-oz cans to-
2 three-oz cans broiled mush-	mato soup
rooms, sliced	2 six-oz cans tomato paste
	1 green pepper, cut up

Simmer ½ hour. Pour over chicken. Refrigerate or freeze. When ready to serve bring to room temperature, cover casserole and bake at 350° F for 1½ hours. Uncover for last 20 minutes. Serve on rice or spaghetti.

Chicken Kiev

*#1   *4 servings*

Warn your guests about the beautiful spurt of butter when they cut into chicken.

Skin and bone

8 halves of chicken breasts

Be careful not to break the flesh. Place each breast between 2 sheets of waxed paper and pound thin. Do not let flesh split. Cut

5 oz chilled butter

into 8 finger-shaped pieces. Place in middle of each breast, sprinkle with

Salt and pepper   Chives

and roll up breasts, being sure to seal the sides as you roll. Dust each roll with

Flour (use about ⅓ cup total)

Dip in

2 lightly beaten eggs

Roll in

1⅓ cups bread crumbs

Refrigerate at least 1 hour to make crumbs stick or freeze. To serve, defrost. In electric skillet, heat to 360° F salad oil, enough to fill half way up.

Fry each piece 7 to 10 minutes on each side. Drain thoroughly on absorbent paper and serve.

Chicken Livers and Mushrooms

*#1   *4 servings*

Shake

1 lb chicken livers

in bag containing

Flour   Salt and pepper

Sauté in

2 tablespoons butter

Then sauté in same pan

2 sliced onions   ½ lb mushrooms

Meanwhile make sauce of

1 chicken bouillon cube   1 teaspoon sugar
1 cup boiling water   1 tablespoon parsley,
1 tablespoon Worcester-   minced
shire sauce

Add livers and mushrooms. Refrigerate or freeze. When ready to serve, return to room temperature; reheat slowly and serve on rice.

Chicken Tetrazzini

*#2   *8 servings*

Worth every bit of work.

Simmer until tender, 1¼ to 1½ hours

5 lb roasting chicken

or 45 to 60 minutes

2 two and a half-lb broilers-fryers, cut up

in

4 cups hot water   3 stalks celery
2½ teaspoons salt   1½ teaspoons onion salt
2 onions   1 teaspoon celery seed
4 carrots   1 teaspoon poultry seasoning

Cool. Remove meat in big pieces. Set aside. Also set aside 2 cups stock. Add rest of stock to

Enough water to make 6   3 tablespoons salt
quarts

When boiling add

1¼ lbs spaghettini

Cook 6 minutes. Drain, place in bottom of large baking dish.

In skillet melt

4 tablespoons butter

Sauté until soft

¾ lb mushrooms, sliced

Sprinkle with

1½ tablespoons lemon juice   ¾ teaspoon salt

Sauté

½ cup sliced almonds

Pour mushrooms and almonds over spaghettini.

Melt, then remove from heat

4 tablespoons butter

Add and blend

2 tablespoons flour   ½ teaspoon pepper
¼ teaspoon paprika   ⅛ teaspoon nutmeg
1½ teaspoons salt

Stir in slowly

¼ cup dry sherry   2 cups chicken broth

Cook and stir until thickened. Remove from heat. Add

1 cup heavy cream

Mix with chicken. Place on top of spaghettini. Refrigerate or freeze. When ready to serve, bring to room temperature, sprinkle with

1 cup Parmesan cheese,   Paprika
grated

Bake at 350° F about ½ to ¾ hour.

Chicken with Almonds

*#1   *4 servings*

Brown

3 lb chicken, cut up

in

6 tablespoons butter

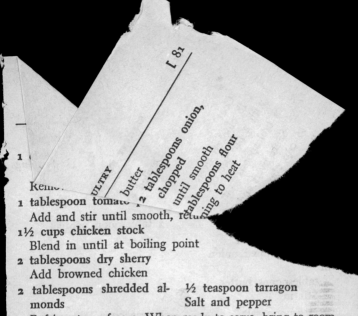

1

Remo...

ULTRY

butter

2 tablespoons onion, chopped

until smooth

tablespoons flour

coming to heat

1 tablespoon tomato

Add and stir until smooth, returning

1½ cups chicken stock
Blend in until at boiling point

2 tablespoons dry sherry
Add browned chicken

2 tablespoons shredded al-
monds　　　　**½ teaspoon tarragon**
　　　　　　　　Salt and pepper

Refrigerate or freeze. When ready to serve, bring to room temperature, cover and cook slowly 45–50 minutes. Arrange chicken in shallow casserole. Stir in

¾ cup sour cream
Pour sauce over chicken. Sprinkle with

1 tablespoon grated cheese
Brown under broiler.

Cold Deviled Chicken

#1　　　　　　　　　　　　　　　　　　6 *servings*

Split in half or into serving pieces

3 two and a half-lb broilers or fryers
Brush both sides with lots of

Melted butter　　　　　**Salt and pepper**

Place skin side down in broiler for about 20–25 minutes. Baste often with butter. Turn and broil 10 more minutes. Put in 400° F oven 10–15 minutes and baste.

Cream together

5 tablespoons dry mustard　　**4 oz stale beer or water**
Spoon generously over chickens. Roll in

1 cup seasoned bread crumbs
Sprinkle with

¼ lb melted butter
Broil 5 minutes until golden. Serve warm or cold.

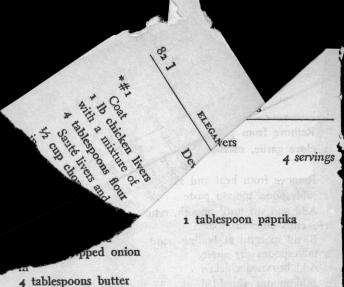

*#1
Coat chicken livers
1 lb chicken livers
with a mixture of
4 tablespoons flour
Sauté livers and
½ cup cho

ELEGA...ers

Dev

4 *servings*

1 tablespoon paprika

...pped onion

4 tablespoons butter
Stir in

½ teaspoon salt
Dash pepper
Dash cayenne
1 teaspoon dry mustard

2 teaspoons Worcester-
shire sauce
1 cup catsup and chili sauce
combined
1 cup water

Refrigerate or freeze. When ready to serve, return to room
temperature; heat through completely.

Duckling in Wine and Liqueur

#1   4 to 6 *servings*
Wash thoroughly inside and out
2 four and a half- to five-lb ducklings
Dry and rub cavities with
Lemon juice
Put in each cavity
A few celery leaves   1 onion sliced
Place ducks, breast side up, on rack in shallow roasting
pan; prick breasts to release fat and roast at 325° F for ½
hour.
Drain fat from pan and add
3 cups white wine
Baste ducks and cook for 1½ hours, basting every 20.

minutes. About 15 minutes before finishing, baste ducks with
2 tablespoons honey

Skim off all fat and add to juices remaining

4 tablespoons butter   2 small cloves garlic,
Grated rind of 2 oranges   crushed
1 cup sliced mushrooms

Bring mixture to boil and simmer gently for 2 minutes.
Remove pan from heat and blend in
6 tablespoons flour

Stir in

½ cup dry sherry   ½ cup Cointreau
½ cup brandy   ½–⅔ cup orange juice

Return pan to heat and stir mixture until smooth and
thick. Add

2 tablespoons currant jelly   2 tablespoons truffle, finely
                                           chopped (definitely op-
                                           tional!)

Discard garlic and season to taste with
Salt and pepper

Use
Few drops red food coloring
to bring to reddish color. Cut ducks in quarters and refrigerate in sauce until serving time. To serve, reheat ducks in
sauce thoroughly. Arrange ducks on serving platter, mask
with sauce and garnish with

Sautéed whole mushroom   Slices of orange
   caps

Orange Chicken Salad

#1   4–6 servings

Combine and chill

4 cups diced cooked chicken   1 cup walnuts, chopped
   meat   1 cup orange sections
2 cups thinly sliced celery

DRESSING

Fold together

¼ cup thawed frozen orange juice concentrate	¼ teaspoon hot pepper sauce
¼ cup mayonnaise	1 cup heavy cream, whipped
Grated rind of 1 orange	

Toss dressing with salad just before serving.

Serve on

Crisp greens

Paella

#1   4 servings

A traditional Spanish delight.

Simmer for two hours

1 five-lb fowl or roasting chicken

Reserve broth. Skin, bone, and dice chicken. In large frying pan place

3 tablespoons olive oil	Diced chicken

Fry until chicken begins to brown, then add

1 large onion, diced	1 clove garlic, crushed

Let onions become transparent, add

2 tomatoes, skinned and mashed	Pinch of saffron (that has been dissolved in 1 teaspoon hot water)
	1 cup chicken broth

Simmer 10 minutes. Add

Salt to taste	1 ten-oz package frozen peas
1 cup canned clam juice	

Bring to boil. Then add

1 lb raw shrimp, peeled

In another pan heat

1 tablespoon olive oil	1 cup raw rice

Stir until rice is well coated. Add to frying pan.

Stir in

12 medium cherrystone clams (in shells)

Boil 10 minutes. At this point you may refrigerate or freeze. To serve return to room temperature and simmer 15 minutes or until heated through.

Decorate with
Sliced pimiento

Rock Cornish Hen with Cherry-Orange Sauce
#1   4 servings

DRESSING

Brown
1 small onion, diced
in
2 tablespoons butter
Add and cook 5 minutes
⅓ cup ham, diced   **⅓ cup mushroom, diced**
Add and mix well
¾ cup cooked wild rice
Use this dressing to stuff
4 individual Rock Cornish hens

SAUCE

Mix together
4 teaspoons cornstarch   **¼ teaspoon dry mustard**
4 tablespoons sugar   **¼ teaspoon ginger**
¼ teaspoon salt
Drain
1 one-lb can red sour, pitted cherries, water packed
Add cherry liquid to cornstarch mixture with

1 tablespoon slivered orange   **¼ cup currant jelly**
rind   **Red food coloring**
½ cup orange juice
Place over medium heat and cook, stirring constantly, until mixture boils and thickens. Add
Drained cherries   **2 tablespoons dry sherry**
When ready to serve, bring to room temperature; bake hens in shallow casserole at 350° F for 45–60 minutes. Baste

often with butter. Just before serving, reheat sauce and
serve in sauce dish with hens.

This sauce is also excellent with crisply roasted duckling.

Southwestern Chicken Salad

#1   *4 servings*

Combine

2 cups cooked white chicken meat, in small cubes	12 small cucumber balls
½ cup celery, chopped	Sections from 1 pink grapefruit
½ cup green pepper, skinned, thinly shredded	

Add

½ cup French dressing

Toss and chill. Press out excess moisture. Toss again with

½ cup mayonnaise	1 tablespoon parsley, minced
1 tablespoon onion, grated	1 tablespoon chives, minced

When ready to serve, line salad bowl with watercress.
Dust salad with

Paprika	Cinnamon
Chopped parsley	Curry

Sprinkle with

2 tablespoons drained capers

Spiced Peaches and Chicken

*#1   *6 servings*

Combine and cook slowly for 10 minutes

1 cup orange juice	2 tablespoons vinegar
1½ cup sliced canned or frozen peaches	1 teaspoon nutmeg
	1 teaspoon basil
2 tablespoons brown sugar	1 clove garlic, minced

Coat

2 two and a half-lb chickens, cut up

in

½ cup flour	Salt and pepper

Brown chicken on both sides in
Oil to depth of ½ inch in 12-inch frying pan
Pour off oil. Pour sauce over chicken. Refrigerate or freeze.
When ready to serve, bring to room temperature, cover and
simmer 20–30 minutes.

Crab and Clam Dip

#1

Blend

6 oz cream cheese   ¼ cup French dressing
4 tablespoons soft butter

Add

1 ten and a half-oz can   Eight-oz can shredded crab-
drained minced clams   meat

Mix lightly. Season to taste with

Worcestershire sauce   Hot pepper sauce

Refrigerate. Serve with crackers. (This can also be spread on toasted rye and placed under broiler until bubbly.)

Curried Cheese Roll

*#3

Put through meat grinder alternately

1 lb sharp cheddar cheese   1 clove garlic
1 cup pecans, unsalted   Dash cayenne pepper
1 three-oz package cream
cheese

Thoroughly mix. Roll into 1-inch cylinders. Roll in

Curry powder

Wrap waxed paper around rolls. Refrigerate at least 2 hours. Let guests slice and spread on rye rounds.

Curried Chicken Balls

*#1   5 dozen

Something different for leftover chicken.

Thoroughly cream

½ lb cream cheese   4 tablespoons mayonnaise

Add

2 cups cooked chicken,   3 tablespoons chutney,
chopped   chopped
1½ cups blanched almonds,   1 teaspoon salt
chopped   2 teaspoons curry powder

Shape into walnut-sized balls. Roll each ball in
1 cup grated coconut
Chill until ready to serve.

Curry Almond Spread

*#3   *2 cups*

Mix together

16 oz soft cream cheese   ½ teaspoon dry mustard
½ cup chopped chutney   ½ cup toasted chopped al-
2 teaspoons curry powder   monds

Refrigerate for several hours, at least. Spread on party rye
or crackers.

Fruit-of-the-Sea Dip

#3   *3½ to 4 cups*

*Improves upon standing . . . prepare at least a day in
advance.*

Combine

1 cup mayonnaise   1½ tablespoons lemon juice
6 tablespoons chili sauce   2 tablespoons pickle relish
1 teaspoon grated onion   2 tablespoons catsup
1 tablespoon Worcestershire   2 tablespoons heavy cream
  sauce

Add

1 lb finely cut-up, cooked shrimp
Serve with crackers, potato chips.

Green Onion Dip

#2   *1 pint*

A quickie, quickie . . .
Mix together

1 pint sour cream   1 envelope green onion dip
Refrigerate. Serve with potato chips or crackers.

Mare's Cheese-Egg Dip

#2

Soften

1 three-oz package chive cream cheese

Stir in

2 tablespoons mayonnaise   ⅛ teaspoon pepper
1 teaspoon prepared   1 teaspoon Worcestershire
  mustard   sauce
¼ teaspoon salt

Add

2 hard-boiled eggs, well chopped

Gradually beat in

2 to 4 tablespoons milk

Refrigerate until ½ hour before serving.

Sprinkle with

Paprika

Serve with crackers, potato chips.

Mystery Cheese Ball

*#3   *3–5 balls*

Will feed an army.

Leave at room temperature and then whirl in the electric mixer

2 lbs Old English cheese   8 oz package cream cheese
5 oz jar bleu cheese spread

Mix, then roll into 3 or 4 large balls. Roll each ball in

Chopped walnuts or pecans

Refrigerate or freeze. Serve at room temperature with crackers.

Mystery Spread

#3

Try this one—an unbelievable combination.

Put through grinder

1 three-oz can pimiento   1 seven-oz can salted peanuts

Mix with
1 tablespoon mayonnaise
Refrigerate at least 2 hours. Serve with crackers.

Pâté de Maison

#3   *one 9x5" loaf*

The real McCoy and very easy to put together.

Mix together

2 lbs calf's liver, uncooked, ground   2 lbs sausage meat, well seasoned, uncooked
                                          Plenty of salt and pepper

Grease well a 9x5-inch loaf mold (same as bread pan). Line it with
Uncooked bacon

Have slices touching each other but not overlapping. Fill mold with half the meat mixture.

Cut lengthwise
2 hard-boiled eggs

Arrange down center of mold. Place on top in latticework design julienned slices of

6 oz liverwurst sausage   6 whole chicken livers, uncooked
6 oz cooked ham
6 oz cooked tongue

Cover with rest of meat mixture and fold over ends of the bacon slices. Cover the whole with waxed paper. Put the mold in a pan of water and bake for 1½ hours in a 350° F oven. Remove from oven and water; weight pâté with heavy object. Cool and refrigerate. To serve, unmold on bed of greens, cut in thin slices and serve with Melba toast.

Pâté en Gelee

#2   *fills 1½-quart mold*

Will fool the most discriminating gourmet . . .

Mix together

2 cans liver pâté   6 oz cream cheese
1 four and a half-oz can   Worcestershire sauce to
  deviled ham   taste

Dissolve

1 envelope gelatin

in

½ cup cold water

Add gelatin to

1 cup beef consomme   ¼ cup dry sherry

which have been heated together. Pour small amount gelatin mixture into bottom of 1½-quart mold. When almost set arrange on bottom

Sliced stuffed olives

Pour remaining gelatin mixture into mold. Let it set. Put pâté mixture on top. Refrigerate. When ready to serve, unmold and serve with party rye or crackers.

Pickled Shrimp

#7   *about 4 dozen shrimp*

Marvelous and low calorie too.

Combine and mix well

1¼ cup salad oil   2½ tablespoons capers and
¾ cup vinegar   juice
1½ teaspoons salt   Dash hot pepper sauce
2½ teaspoons celery seed

Pour sauce over

2 lbs shrimp, cooked and cleaned

Place in shallow dish in which the shrimp may be served. Cover with

1 onion, thinly sliced in rings

Add

2–3 bay leaves

Cover and store in refrigerator at least 24 hours. Drain and
serve. Will keep 1 week in refrigerator.

Pickles and Peanuts

#3

Crazy but good.

Whip together

1 eight-oz package cream
cheese

½ cup salted peanuts,
chopped *very fine*

½ cup chopped sweet gher-
kins

1 teaspoon seasoned salt

1 teaspoon minced parsley

Put into crocks ready to serve. Refrigerate. Serve with
crackers.

Plaza Dip

#2

Blend together and chill at least 2 hours

1½ cups sour cream

½ cup mayonnaise

1 teaspoon dry mustard

1 tablespoon horseradish

1 clove garlic, crushed

2 tablespoons chili sauce

2 tablespoons anchovy paste

2 hard-boiled eggs, chopped

1 green pepper, chopped

1 tablespoon chopped parsley

Serve with chips or crackers.

Raw Vegetables with Dip

#1

For the diet-conscious.

Clean, cut up, and wrap securely

Carrot sticks

Raw cauliflowerettes

Radish roses

Cucumber sticks

DIP (#2)

Mix together

1 pint sour cream
1⅓ tablespoons white horseradish
1 tablespoon paprika
1 tablespoon minced chives

1 teaspoon salt
1 teaspoon tarragon
¼ teaspoon MSG
1 clove garlic, crushed
⅛ teaspoon pepper

Chill thoroughly. Surround bowl with vegetables.

Shrimp Cocktail Sauce

#1   *1 cup, 6 servings*

Foolproof sauce.

Combine

⅓ cup chili sauce
⅓ cup catsup
3 tablespoons horseradish
4 tablespoons lemon juice

2 teaspoons Worcestershire
  sauce
Dash salt
Dash hot pepper sauce

When ready to serve, divide

1 lb cooked shrimp

into 6 servings and place on crisp lettuce leaves. Spoon sauce over all.

Shrimp Mix

#1

Blend together

8 oz cream cheese

8 tablespoons mayonnaise

Mix in

2 tablespoons Worcester-
  shire sauce
2 tablespoons onion juice
2 diced fresh tomatoes

½ lb cut-up cooked shrimp
(1 teaspoon red horseradish,
  if desired)

Refrigerate. Serve with crackers or chips.

Smoked Salmon Pinwheels

*#1   30 hors d'oeuvres

Spread
8 oz cream cheese
on
½ lb of large thin slices of smoked salmon

Roll up. Refrigerate or freeze. Slice and serve on Melba toast rounds.

Smokey Cheese

#1

A *quickie*.
Combine thoroughly

1 six-oz package smoked   3 tablespoons sparerib sauce
cheese spread

Serve on crackers.

Stix and Stones

*#7   6 quarts

In a large roasting pan mix together

1 six-oz package small cheese   1 eight-oz can walnuts
crackers   2 six-oz cans pecans
2 six-oz packages corn chips   1 three and a half-oz pack-
2 four-oz cans toasted coco-   age popcorn
nut chips

Mix together in saucepan

½ lb melted butter   1 teaspoon curry powder
½ teaspoon garlic salt   6 drops hot pepper sauce
1 clove garlic, crushed   1 tablespoon Worcester-
1 teaspoon salt   shire sauce

Sprinkle liquid mixture through dry mixture. Bake at 250° F for 1 hour, stirring occasionally. This may be made weeks in advance if stored in airtight containers.

Stuffed Rigatoni

#1   *30 hors d'oeuvres*

Cook according to directions on package

30 large rigatoni

Blend

1 three-oz can deviled ham   2 tablespoons mayonnaise
1 five-oz jar pimiento cheese
  spread

Fill each rigatoni with mixture. Insert

Stuffed olives

into one end of each rigatoni. Refrigerate.

Tuna-Cheese Spread

#3

Try it hot too!

Cut into pieces and melt in top of double boiler

1 eight-oz package processed Old English cheese

Remove from heat and add

1 seven-oz can tuna fish   ½ teaspoon Worcestershire
½ cup mayonnaise   sauce

Chill. Serve with crackers.

SAUCE

Combine

3 eggs yolks beaten   3½ tablespoons sugar
Juice of 1½ lemons   ½ tablespoon salt

Add

1 cup strained fish broth

Cook until thick. If more gravy is desired

Add

2 teaspoons cornstarch   ½ cup more broth

Serve sauce cold over cold fish.

Crab-and-Mushroom Casserole

*#1   *4 servings*

Sauté for 5 minutes

1 lb sliced mushrooms

in

2 tablespoons butter
Melt

6 tablespoons butter
Blend in

⅓ cup flour

Add and cook until thickened

1 ten-oz can chicken broth   Salt and pepper to taste
1½ cups medium or light
cream

In 6-cup casserole arrange in alternate layers

Mushrooms   1 lb crabmeat
Sauce

Sprinkle with

Buttered crumbs   Grated American cheese

Refrigerate or freeze. To serve, bring to room temperature
and put casserole in 350° F oven and bake about 30 minutes.

Crabmeat Mandarin

#1   4 *servings*

Cut in half lengthwise

2 small pineapples

Scoop out the inside, leaving ½ inch rim and cut insides into bite-size pieces.

Combine and mix well

1 cup mayonnaise

1 to 2 teaspoons curry powder

Add and mix well

1 lb crabmeat, flaked

2 eleven-oz cans mandarin
oranges, drained

3 heaping tablespoons chutney solids, chopped

2 tablespoons lemon juice

Pineapple

Chill. Liquid will accumulate and should be drained off before placing in pineapple shells, just before serving.

Filet of Flounder with Grapes

#1   4 *servings*

Sauté until tender

½ lb sliced mushrooms

in

3 tablespoons butter

Season with salt and pepper.

Poach in large skillet

2 lbs flounder or sole filets

in

1 cup milk

Simmer 5–10 minutes according to thickness of filet. Season with salt and pepper. Remove filets carefully.

In saucepan melt

4 tablespoons butter

Remove from fire and add

1½ tablespoons flour

Slowly add milk from poaching. Add

2 tablespoons Parmesan   ½ cup light cream
cheese, grated

Return to fire and stir until it thickens.

Arrange fish, mushrooms, and

½ lb seedless green grapes

in layers in buttered casserole. Cover with sauce and sprinkle with

Parmesan cheese

Refrigerate. When ready to serve, return to room temperature; bake at 400° F for 15 minutes.

Filet of Sole with Crabmeat Sauce
#1   *4 servings*

In saucepan melt

1½ tablespoons butter

Stir in

1 tablespoon flour

Add

½ teaspoon salt   Pinch onion salt
½ teaspoon lemon juice   Dash hot pepper sauce
¼ teaspoon prepared horse-   ⅛ teaspoon MSG
radish   Dash pepper
⅛ teaspoon Worcestershire
sauce

Blend in

⅓ cup milk

Cook until thick, stirring constantly. Remove from heat. Add

1 cup crabmeat

Arrange in greased shallow casserole

2 filets of sole

Pour over them crabmeat mixture. Top with

2 more filets of sole.

Combine and pour over filets

2 tablespoons melted butter

1½ teaspoons lemon juice

Sprinkled with paprika. When ready to serve bake at 350°
F for 30 minutes. Serve with lemon wedges.

Hawaiian Shrimp Curry

*#2   6 servings

Sauté until golden

2 medium onions, chopped

in

2 tablespoons butter

Make a paste of

7 tablespoons flour	1½ teaspoon sugar
1 tablespoon curry powder	¼ teaspoon powdered ginger
1½ teaspoon salt	½ cup chicken bouillon

Combine this with onion and

2 cups milk	½ cup chicken bouillon

Cook over low heat until thick. Meanwhile cook in boiling water for 2 minutes

2 cucumbers, peeled, cut in 2½-inch strips

Drain cucumbers and drop into sauce with

2 lbs shrimp, cooked and cleaned	1 tablespoon onion, minced

When ready to serve, return to room temperature; reheat
and serve hot with Coconut Rice (see Vegetables, p. 125).

Lobster Curry

*#1   4 servings

In

2 tablespoons butter

Sauté

1 cup onions, chopped	¼ cup carrots, grated
½ cup celery, chopped	1 clove garlic, crushed
½ cup apples, chopped	

When tender add

2 tablespoons curry powder   ¼ teaspoon ginger
1 tablespoon flour   1¼ cups chicken stock

Simmer for 20 minutes. Put through blender. Add

¼ cup heavy cream   1 ten-oz package frozen peas
2 cups cooked lobtser meat   Salt to taste

Simmer for 5 minutes, until heated through.

If dish is to be frozen, do not add peas until just before reheating. Serve with Coconut Rice (see Vegetables, p. 125).

Lobster Macaroni Imperial

*#1   4 servings

Heat together

½ cup butter   ½ teaspoon Worcestershire
¼ teaspoon dry mustard   sauce
½ 14-oz bottle catsup

Make layers in casserole of

½ lb elbow macaroni,   1 lb lobster meat
  cooked and drained   ½ lb sharp cheddar cheese,
Sauce as above   grated

Refrigerate or freeze. When ready to serve return to room temperature and place casserole in pan of hot water and bake at 350° F for 45 minutes.

Margaret's Shrimp Mold

#2   8 servings

Heat

2 ten and a half-oz cans cream of tomato soup
  add

2½ envelopes unflavored gelatin
which has been diluted in
¼ cup cold water

Add

12 ounces cream cheese, softened	2 cups celery, finely chopped
2 cups mayonnaise	1 cucumber, diced
1 green pepper, finely chopped	2 teaspoons onion, grated

Place in 6-cup ring mold and jell. To serve, unmold and fill center with

1½ lbs cooked, peeled shrimp

that has been marinated in

French dressing

Top with

Thousand Island dressing

Garnish platter with

Hard cooked eggs   Watercress
Tomatoes, sliced

THOUSAND ISLAND DRESSING (#3)

Combine

1 cup mayonnaise	1 tablespoon green pepper, chopped
4 teaspoons chili sauce	
1 tablespoon chives	3 tablespoons red pepper, chopped
1 teaspoon tarragon vinegar	
	1 teaspoon paprika

Refrigerate. Within 4 hours of serving add

½ cup heavy cream, whipped

Piquant Crab Casserole

*#1   4 servings

An unusual combination with delightful results.

Cook, according to directions on package

2 ten-oz packages frozen spinach, chopped

Drain well and spread in greased 2-quart casserole. Sprinkle with

1 cup American sharp cheese, grated	1 pound crabmeat
	2 tablespoons lemon juice

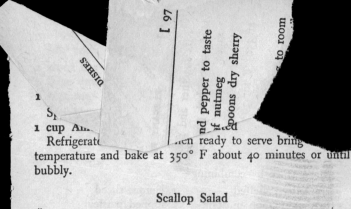

DISHES

1

S

1 cup A...

... nd pepper to taste
... of nutmeg
... poons dry sherry
... to room

Refrigerate ... ...en ready to serve bring ...
temperature and bake at 350° F about 40 minutes or until
bubbly.

Scallop Salad

#1   4 servings

In a skillet combine and bring to a boil

½ cup white wine   3 sprigs parsley
¼ cup water   Pinch tarragon
1 onion, peeled

Add

1½ lbs scallops

Simmer 3–4 minutes for sea scallops, 1½ minutes for bay
scallops.

Cool in broth until ready to use. For salad, combine

Scallops, drained   12 sliced green olives
½ lb whole mushroom caps,   Mayonnaise to moisten
  steamed

Scalloped Oysters

#1   6 servings

Mix together

⅔ cup melted butter   3 cups coarse, soda cracker
                                   crumbs

Drain, reserving ¼ cup of the liquor

3 dozen shucked oysters

Arrange in a shallow 1½-quart baking dish, alternate layers
of crackers and oysters, finishing with top layer of crumbs.

Sprinkle with

2 teaspoons salt   ¼ teaspoon pepper

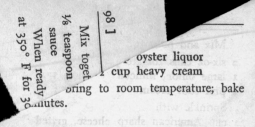

Mix toget...
⅛ teaspoon
sauce
When ready
at 350° F for 30...

oyster liquor
½ cup heavy cream
bring to room temperature; bake
...nutes.

Scampi

Make sauce by combining

½ lb butter, melted
1 teaspoon Dijon mustard
1 teaspoon Worcestershire
  sauce
4 cloves garlic, pressed
½ teaspoon chili powder
  Place on jelly roll pan

1 lemon, sliced
Chopped parsley
Salt
Pepper
Paprika
2 tablespoons white wine

2 lbs shrimp, cooked with tail shell left on

Pour sauce over shrimp and let stand at least 24 hours in refrigerator. When ready to serve, bake at 350° F for 20 minutes, basting often. Place under broiler for a minute or two until tails turn brown.

Seashore Casserole

Sauté together

½ lb lobster meat
½ lb cooked shrimp
in

½ lb crabmeat
1 tablespoon onion, minced

¼ cup butter
  Melt in small saucepan
3 tablespoons butter
  Add and heat
3 tablespoons flour
  Add gradually, stirring until thick
1½ cups milk

Fold seafood mixture into this sauce. Then add

2 teaspoons prepared mustard

1 tablespoon Worcestershire sauce

1 tablespoon onion, minced
Dash hot pepper sauce
Salt and pepper
2 tablespoons dry sherry

Refrigerate or freeze. When ready to serve, return to room temperature; heat in top of double boiler and serve over rice, noodles, or pastry shells or place in casserole, sprinkle with bread crumbs and cheese. Bake at 400° F 12–15 minutes.

Shrimp-and-Cheese Delight

*#1   *4 servings*

Sauté for 5 minutes

¼ lb mushrooms, sliced

in

2 tablespoons butter
Lightly mix in

½ lb cooked shrimp
1½ cups cooked rice
1½ cup grated American cheese
½ cup milk

3 tablespoons catsup
½ teaspoon Worcestershire sauce
¼ teaspoon salt
⅛ teaspoon pepper

Pour into 2-quart casserole. Refrigerate or freeze. When ready to bake bring to room temperature and place in 350° F oven for 25 minutes or until bubbly.

Shrimp-Stuffed Filets

#1   *4 servings*

Sauté

⅔ cup celery, finely chopped

in

2 tablespoons butter
Combine with

1 lb shrimp, cooked and chopped

1 large onion, finely chopped

½ cup flavored bread crumbs
1 egg, slightly beaten

Spread on

8 thin flounder or sole filets

Roll up and place in lightly greased baking dish. Pour following sauce over filets. Then top with

Buttered bread crumbs   **Chopped parsley**
Grated Swiss or Parmesan
  cheese

Refrigerate. When ready to serve bake in 350° F oven 20–30 minutes.

SAUCE

Empty into saucepan

1 package mushroom soup mix

Gradually stir in

2 cups cold water

Heat until boiling.

Add

¼ cup dry white wine

Pour over filets.

Sour Cream Shrimp Curry

#1   *4 servings*

In

2 tablespoons butter

sauté until tender, but not brown

⅓ cup chopped onion   **1 clove garlic, minced**
¼ cup chopped green pep-
  per

Stir in

1 cup sour cream   **¼ teaspoon salt**
1 teaspoon curry powder   **Pepper**

Add

1¼ lbs shrimp, cooked

Refrigerate. When ready to serve, reheat slowly, stirring and serve with rice.